keeping it simple

Gary Rhodes

Photography by Noel Murphy

For my sons, Samuel and George, my greatest food critics,
who bring me laughter, love and happiness

MICHAEL JOSEPH

Penguin Books Ltd, Registered
Offices: 80 Strand, London
WC2R ORL, England

www.penguin.com

First published 2005

7

Text copyright ©
Gary Rhodes, 2005

Photography copyright ©
Noel Murphy, 2005

Design copyright ©
Kysen, 2005

Published by the Penguin Group

Penguin Books Ltd, 80 Strand, London WC2R 0RL, England

Penguin Group (USA) Inc., 375 Hudson Street, New York, New York 10014, USA

Penguin Group (Canada), 90 Eglinton Avenue East, Suite 700, Toronto, Ontario,
  Canada M4P 3YZ (a division of Pearson Penguin Canada Inc.)

Penguin Ireland, 25 St Stephen's Green, Dublin 2, Ireland
  (a division of Penguin Books Ltd)

Penguin Group (Australia), 250 Camberwell Road, Camberwell, Victoria 3124,
  Australia (a division of Pearson Australia Group Pty Ltd)

Penguin Books India Pvt Ltd, 11 Community Centre,
  Panchsheel Park, New Delhi – 110 017, India

Penguin Group (NZ), cnr Airborne and Rosedale Roads, Albany,
  Auckland 1310, New Zealand (a division of Pearson New Zealand Ltd)

Penguin Books (South Africa) (Pty) Ltd, 24 Sturdee Avenue,
  Rosebank 2196, South Africa

Colour Reproduction by Dot Gradations Ltd, UK

Printed in Italy by Graphicom

A CIP catalogue record for this book is available from the British Library

ISBN-13: 978–0–718–14621–4

ISBN-10: 0–718–14621–2

contents

introduction

This is the book I've wanted to write for so many years, one that isn't dictated or overly influenced by my thirty years in professional kitchens. Yes, there are bits and pieces of that here, but generally I'm just sharing with you the foods and dishes I like to cook at home.

Good cooking doesn't have to consist of lots of expensive ingredients; 'the simpler the better' couldn't be more accurate. It's important to remember, however, that quality ingredients are the essence of good food. These hold so much flavour, which means they don't have to rely on overcomplicated cooking. Quite a variety of ingredients feature in these pages; most are cheap and easy to find, but none of the recipes are set in stone. Follow your own instincts and use this book as a guide from which to discover and create your own favourites, treating the recipes as a sort of pick 'n' mix, swapping and changing ingredients where it suits.

You'll also discover that there are degrees of simplicity to choose from, as some of the recipes are easier than others. The best way to judge is to check the length of the recipe. A recipe with just two or three points indicates something very simple. But don't be put off by a long list of ingredients. With a closer look, you'll notice that many of these are just basics, such as olive oil, butter, eggs, milk, salt, pepper and lemon juice.

The first chapter shows you what I like to keep in my cupboards and fridge. This collection appears time and time again throughout the book and can be a helpful guide to keep your weekly shopping list a little bit shorter.

I want you to enjoy cooking and eating from this collection as much as I do. I hope it shows that most chefs prefer to keep their cooking at home simple and unpretentious. Time for cooking can be limited, so just choose the best ingredients and don't overplay them. It's all about keeping it simple.

my kitchen

The key to simple cooking is a fridge and cupboard well stocked with the basics, which just need topping up with the freshest fish and meat, vegetables and fruit.

my fridge and freezer

Bacon, diced pancetta or sliced ham

Butter. Like most chefs, I generally use unsalted butter when I'm cooking, to give me total control over the seasoning. However, this is not essential, so use whatever you have.

Cheese. Cheddar, Parmesan and mozzarella are always in my fridge.

Crème fraîche, sour cream or natural yoghurt. These all have a long shelf-life and are useful when you want to add just a spoonful to a sauce.

Eggs. All the eggs I use are free range.

Mayonnaise. Making your own is wonderful, but I also have a lot of respect for good-quality bought mayonnaise.

Parma ham

Peas

Pesto

Ready-made puff and shortcrust pastry

Soy sauce. This is best refrigerated once opened.

Vanilla ice cream

my cupboard

Caster and demerara sugar

Cocoa powder and instant coffee

Custard powder

Dried herbs and spices. I don't like to keep a lot because they don't retain their freshness for long. A jar of mixed herbs is perhaps the only essential dried herb, while cayenne pepper and paprika are the two spices I rely on. Green peppercorns are a useful standby, especially for steak, and I like to have a whole nutmeg for grating into puddings or sauces.

Dried pasta. You can use any shape with any sauce, so buy whatever you like.

Golden syrup and black treacle

Lobster bisque. A very useful soup to keep on hand for making an instant fish or seafood sauce.

Mustard. I always have English, Dijon and wholegrain, but you can use whatever you prefer.

Oils. Olive oil is an essential. You also need a basic oil for cooking at higher temperatures. Vegetable, groundnut or sunflower oils are all good choices.

Passata. This is your instant tomato sauce.

Plain and self-raising flour

Plain chocolate. Whether this is an extra or an essential depends on you!

Redcurrant jelly. I like this for enhancing sauces, often adding a dollop to slightly sweeten my gravies.

Rice. Long-grain, basmati and arborio rices are the only ones we have at home.

Salt and pepper. I use both coarse sea salt and table salt in my cooking. I also prefer the taste and texture of white pepper to black, but use whatever you prefer.

Stock cubes. Home-made stock is lovely, but it's certainly not quick and simple to make, and these days there are lots of instant varieties on offer. Try one of the tubs of liquid stocks available in the chilled cabinets or a tin of consommé, which provides the richest of flavours. Consommé is also clarified, giving a shiny finish to sauces and gravies. Beef is the easiest to get hold of and it suits most meat and chicken dishes, while game consommé is the one to use for game dishes and duck.

If you're making stock using cubes, look for the rectangular ones with a paste-like texture, rather than the crumbly cubes, and add just half a cube to the recommended water quantity for a fresher, less artificial flavour. For a clear finish, boil the water in a saucepan, whisk in the cube and simmer for 1–2 minutes to clarify.

Tabasco and Worcestershire sauces

Tin of chopped tomatoes. One of the most useful cupboard standbys of all. In the summer, you can substitute about six large fresh tomatoes for a tin. Peel them first, following the method in the recipe for fiery tomato sauce on page 319.

White wine vinegar. This is the vinegar I use for general cooking. Red wine vinegar is also a favourite, especially one that bears the hallmark of a good wine, such as a Cabernet Sauvignon. Balsamic vinegar is a delicious extra, and the older it is, the better the flavour.

Walnut, hazelnut or sesame oil. I like to have some flavoured oils to add a twist to my salad dressings.

Vanilla extract or vanilla pods

useful extra utensils

Balloon whisk

Colander

Fine cheese grater

Fine strainer

Fish slice

Juicer

Knife sharpener

Mandolin slicer

Measuring spoons

Non-stick frying pan and an omelette pan

Nutmeg grater

Pastry brush

Rubber spatula

Tongs

Tweezers

Wok

fish seafood poultry pork lamb beef vegetables pasta and rice eggs and cheese desserts

keeping fish simple

All my fish recipes are about experimenting with different flavours, textures and styles. If you see a recipe you really love, but you're not keen on that fish, use another. What's most important is not what it says in the recipe, but what catches your eye in the shop. The freshest produce will need the least help and that's what leads to simpler cooking.

how to choose fish

At the fish counter:

Look first at the marble slab and always give priority to the fish.

Don't be afraid of substitutions. The golden rule is to make sure you buy the freshest fish available, which can often mean changing your menu plans at the last moment. A flat fish will adapt to any of the cod recipes. If turbot is too expensive, don't feel you can't do the recipe with another flat fish or even haddock or salmon.

Don't mock frozen fish. Often frozen aboard ship within hours of being caught, they are a great alternative to fresh fish.

If you do make the trip to a good fishmonger, buy a lot. Save something for supper and freeze the rest. If the fish is really fresh, it will cook up beautifully once defrosted.

For the simplest cooking, buy fish that has been filleted for you; it's rare the fishmonger refuses. However, if you've bought fillets, do quickly check that the fine bones have been removed. Run your hand along a fillet and take out any stray bones with tweezers.

How much? If you're buying fillets, 175–225g (6–8oz) is enough per person for a main course. For whole fish, a general rule is that flat ones carry 50 per cent flesh to bone, while the majority of round fish offer 60–70 per cent. I suggest 375–450g (13oz–1lb) per person.

A freshness checklist:

Smell: Fresh fish has a salty, seaweed aroma. A strong smell of fish spells stale. Don't touch it.

Eyes: Should be clear, bright and full.

Skin: Glistening with clear, not cloudy, slime.

Gills: Bright red or deep pink gills show that oxygen is still present and the fish fresh.

Touch: Firm fish is fresh fish. If you press on the skin, it shouldn't leave a finger mark.

What's best avoided:

As soon as a fish is filleted, it starts to deteriorate. It's best to buy and eat fillets on the same day and if you have a good fishmonger, he can fillet fish on the spot for you. In your supermarket, buy from the fish counter and ask them to cut exactly the pieces you want from their whole fish.

Try to avoid buying your fish on a Monday because that fish was landed at best on Friday.

If you can't eat your fish straight away, try to maximize freshness by placing a J-cloth on a plate, topping with the fish and covering with clingfilm. This prevents the fish soaking up stale juices and water.

cooking your catch

Fish cookery isn't about cooking the flesh right through. All you're really doing is warming up the meat and setting the flakes.

To stay in control of the cooking, once a fillet is two-thirds cooked, turn it over and switch off the heat. By the time you've drained some potatoes and fixed a sauce, the residual heat will have cooked the fish to perfection.

Is it cooked? – a quick test:

Look: The flesh changes colour as the fish cooks. For a fillet, look at the side of the fish to see if it is beginning to turn from translucent to opaque.

Touch: The flesh strengthens when warmed. Perfection is indicated by a press that just gives.

Test: For a whole fish, insert a small knife or skewer into the thickest part. If it slides easily to the bone, the fish is cooked.

keeping pan-frying simple

Why: Fish has got enough personality to speak for itself and at the end of the day, any fish can simply be pan-fried. Grab a pan and you're in business.

Best for: A few small fish or fillets.

I use: A good non-stick frying pan is the number one necessity. If you're cooking for four people, use two.

Prep: Always lightly dust any skinned fish with flour to keep it non-stick too.

Cook: Pan-fry the fish gently over a medium heat, allowing only the slightest colour. If you allow it to go a deep brown, the flesh can become very dry and leathery. I only ever begin pan-frying in oil because butter colours too quickly. When the fish has a golden edge, add a knob of butter.

How long: About 2–7 minutes (depending on the size of the fillets) on one side, then turn the fish, switch off the heat and allow the residual heat to finish the cooking in just a few minutes.

Simplest meal: Pan-fried fish with a handful of capers or halved grapes thrown into the sizzling butter.

keeping roasting simple

Why: Roast if you want a well-coloured, crispy skin. Bake at a lower temperature if you want the fish to take on the influence of other ingredients in the pan.

Best for: Big whole fish.

I use: A roasting pan or an ovenproof frying pan if starting the fish off on top of the stove.

Prep: I'm not a massive fan of scoring fish before roasting because it exposes prime flesh to drying out. For a little protection, brush your fish with olive oil. When baking, other flavours can be scattered in the pan such as shredded fennel, herbs, star anise or a splash of Pernod and water. Rest the fish on top to cook.

Cook: Preheat the oven to about 220°C/425°F/gas 7 for roasting. You can flash-fry your fish in a very hot pan on top of the stove first to start the crisping process. For baking, set the oven at 180°C/350°F/gas 4.

How long: For a 1.35–2.25kg (3–5lb) whole fish, I'd recommend 20–30 minutes.

Simplest meal: Roasted fish with a quick sauce made in the pan from red wine, stirred until it boils down a bit, cream and butter.

keeping grilling simple

Why: This is a healthy way of cooking because you don't need a lot of oil or butter. Instead you are relying on the charcoal or toasted flavours of the fish you gain from the cooking method.

Best for: Oily fish grill particularly well.

I use: A ridged griddle pan or, if you're barbecuing or toasting a whole fish, a wire clamp to hold it.

Prep: If using a griddle pan, preheat to very hot and wipe the pan and the fish with oil. If cooking under the grill, the most important point is to make sure it is well preheated and the fish placed very close to the heat.

Cook: Keep the heat high to cook the fish quickly for a good colour and flavour, rather than allowing it to sweat and lose its juices.

How long: About 4–8 minutes each side for small whole fish, 2–8 minutes on one side only for fillets, such as mackerel and red mullet.

Simplest meal: Chargrilled sole or salmon with a spoonful of mayonnaise or hollandaise mixed with horseradish sauce and snipped chives.

keeping steaming simple

Why: With no additives whatsoever, steaming means you're going to be tasting your fish in its most natural form.

Best for: Fillets because of their small size.

I use: A bamboo or metal steamer. If you don't have a steamer, you can steam in a shallow pan or wok. Just add a couple of centimetres of liquid to come a little way up the fish and use a tightly fitting lid or plate to cover.

Prep: Wrap the fish in buttered parchment, foil or even blanched spinach, lettuce or cabbage leaves to protect its moistness and collect all the juices.

Cook: You don't need the water boiling too rapidly. Steam carries quite a violent heat, so a rapid simmer is perfect.

How long: About 4–10 minutes for fillets.

Simplest meal: Steamed fish and Jersey Royals with a spoonful of buttery, sweet peas.

keeping poaching simple

Why: This is a very classic, simple way to cook fish.

Best for: Almost any fish. Skate tastes surprisingly beautiful poached.

I use: A fish kettle for round fish or a large roasting pan for flat fish.

Cook: The temperature of the water is important. It should just murmur, with the gentlest of bubbles. You can also poach in a stock or wine, and milk is often used for smoked fish to mellow the smokiness.

How long: About 15–25 minutes for whole fish and 8–15 minutes for steaks.

Simplest meal: If you poach over water, it's all about what you serve with the fish. Poached white fish can be a little bland so give it a helping hand with a mayonnaise, mustard, lemon and whipped cream sauce or a dressing of tomatoes with a hint of garlic and fresh herbs.

key flavours for fish

Lemon. Just a little squeeze makes the fish shout louder.

Herbs. Add fresh tarragon, chives or parsley to the pan while you're frying or mix into butter to melt over grilled fish.

Strong flavours. Pickles and relishes are wonderful, but do need to be partnered with a robust cooking method and toned down, even if it is just with a little whipped cream, mayonnaise or hollandaise. Horseradish goes particularly well with grilled or roasted fish and a spoonful of pickle or relish can be served alongside oily fish.

Capers and shallots. Perfect with smoked salmon.

New potatoes. Steamed Jersey Royals are fish's best partner.

Crusty bread and creamy mash. Excellent alternatives to new potatoes.

some simple fish suppers

All-purpose creamy herb sauce. Warm a handful of fresh herbs with some cream and lemon to make an instant sauce.

Grilled salmon with a dill dressing. Salad dressings are wonderful poured over hot fish. Drizzle olive oil, dill and a squeeze of lime over hot grilled salmon.

Smoked fish with a hot mayonnaise. Smoked fish makes the simplest starter when served with a mustard or shallot-flavoured mayonnaise.

Poached salmon with a chilli cucumber relish. Make your own cucumber relish by adding peeled slivers of cucumber to a little white wine vinegar, olive oil, coarse sea salt, twist of pepper and, if you want, fine rings of red chilli. Serve with a piece of poached salmon.

Mushroom wine sauce (for the fish of your choice). A few mushrooms from the bottom of your fridge can be thinly sliced and added with white wine to the cooking juices.

Pan-fried catch of the day with hot garlic spinach. Buy a bag of prepared baby spinach and drop into a wok with some hot oil, mushrooms and a little garlic until just wilted. Serve with any pan-fried fish.

Tuna with a sweetcorn relish. Try a ready-made sweetcorn relish with seared tuna.

Trout with nutty new potatoes. If you are a fan of the classic trout with almonds, try taking some halved hot new potatoes and mixing with a handful of toasted almonds, some olive oil, butter, parsley and lemon. Serve with simple pan-fried trout.

simple sauces for fish

beurre blanc

serves **four–six**

40g (1½oz) shallots,
  finely chopped
2 tablespoons
  white wine vinegar
5 tablespoons
  dry white wine
2 tablespoons double
  cream or crème fraîche
175g (6oz) cold unsalted
  butter, cut into cubes
salt and white pepper

This butter sauce complements almost any fish, whether steamed, poached, baked or pan-fried, as well as pan-fried or grilled chicken. Drizzle over steamed broccoli or any other green vegetables.

- Put the shallots, vinegar and white wine into a small saucepan and simmer until just 1–2 tablespoons of the liquid are left. Whisk in the cream and return to a simmer.

- Over a low heat, whisk in the butter, a few pieces at a time, until completely creamy. It's important not to allow the sauce to boil because this will curdle the butter.

- If the sauce is too thick, a few tablespoons of water can be added to slightly loosen. Season with the salt and freshly ground white pepper.

and more

A squeeze of lemon can be added to sharpen the flavour.

For a smoother consistency, strain the sauce through a sieve.

beurre noisette

serves **four–six**

100g (4oz) butter
juice of 1 lemon
salt and pepper
1 tablespoon
  chopped parsley

This nut-brown butter classically goes with Dover sole, the butter added to the pan the fish has been pan-fried in and cooked until sizzling and a deep golden brown. It can be made at the very last minute or sizzled earlier and reheated to serve with any fried fish.

• Heat the butter in a frying pan until it reaches the nut-brown stage.

• At this point, pour in the lemon juice and season with salt and pepper before adding the parsley and spooning over the fish.

and more

For extra flavour, try adding 1–2 tablespoons of capers, some cooked shrimps or prawns or sliced or quartered mushrooms (which will cook in the butter as it heats up).

nutty beurre vinaigrette

serves **eight**

100g (4oz) butter
3 tablespoons red wine,
  tarragon or sherry vinegar
4–5 tablespoons walnut,
  olive, hazelnut or
  groundnut oil
salt and pepper

I have included here a nut-brown butter vinaigrette, which is a superb alternative to the beurre noisette for salads or warm fish and meat dishes.

- Heat the butter in a frying pan until it reaches the nut-brown stage.

- At this point, remove the pan from the heat and pour in the vinegar. Whisk in the oil, season with salt and pepper and leave to cool.

- The vinaigrette can be stored in a screw-top jar or bottle and refrigerated until needed, serving at room temperature or slightly warm.

quick hollandaise sauce

serves **four–six**

175g (6oz) unsalted butter
2 egg yolks
juice of 1 lemon
salt
a pinch of cayenne pepper

This easy version of the classic French sauce is not served hot, but lukewarm, with grilled, steamed or pan-fried fish, poached eggs or any green vegetables. If clarifying the butter is too much trouble, the butter can be replaced with the same quantity of warm olive oil.

• Melt the butter in a saucepan and simmer for 2 minutes. Remove from the heat and leave to cool until warm. Alternatively, place the butter in a bowl, cover and microwave just until melted. The butter will now have separated, leaving all the milky white solids in the base of the pan and the clear clarified butter on top.

• Place the egg yolks, lemon juice and 2 tablespoons of water in a blender and blend briefly to combine.

• While blending, slowly ladle in just the warm clear butter until it is all incorporated to a thick, creamy consistency. Season with the salt and cayenne pepper and serve just warm.

and more

If making this sauce with olive oil, which tends to thicken quite quickly, loosen the finished sauce with 2–3 tablespoons of water.

Mousseline sauce
With a lighter consistency, this sauce is superb with almost any fish. Fold in 1–2 tablespoons of whipped cream.

Mustard hollandaise
This sauce works well with fish and is beautiful with pork and chicken. Stir a heaped teaspoon or two of English, Dijon or wholegrain mustard into the finished sauce.

Sauce Maltaise
This blood-orange-flavoured classic can be served with grilled fish or fried or grilled chicken.
Boil the finely grated zest of 1 blood orange with the juice from 2 until just 3-4 tablespoons of liquid are left. Whisk into the sauce to finish.

tartare sauce

makes **300ml** (10fl oz)

300ml (10fl oz)
  mayonnaise
1 tablespoon finely
  chopped gherkins
1 tablespoon finely
  chopped capers
1 tablespoon finely
  chopped shallots
  or onion
1 tablespoon chopped
  parsley
salt and pepper

Use this sauce to add a sharp extra bite to fish, fried in particular, or breadcrumbed chicken. The measurements can just be halved to make a smaller quantity.

- Mix together all of the ingredients, seasoning to taste with the salt and pepper.

and more

A squeeze of lemon can also be added to the sauce.

dover sole with hot lemon butter

serves **two**

2 x 450–550g (1–1¼lb)
  Dover soles, filleted
  and skinned
flour, for dusting
olive oil, for cooking
salt and pepper
25g (1oz) butter
4 wedges of lemon

The Dover sole can also be cooked whole and the frying time increased by a few minutes. Either way, cooking fish doesn't get any easier than this.

- Pat the sole fillets dry on kitchen paper before lightly dusting in the flour.

- Heat some olive oil in a large non-stick frying pan. Once the oil is hot, place the fillets in the pan and fry over a medium to high heat, without moving them, for 3–4 minutes until they are a rich golden brown.

- Season the fillets with salt and pepper before adding the butter to the pan and squeezing 2 wedges of lemon juice over them. Turn the fillets, then remove the frying pan from the heat.

- After 1–2 minutes of sitting in the hot pan, the fish are ready to serve. Spoon over the lemon butter and serve with a lemon wedge.

and more

Although Dover sole is listed, lemon sole or plaice makes a very good second choice.

Extra flavours can be added to the lemon butter, sizzling it again just before spooning over the fish. Try a couple of teaspoons of capers or some herbs, such as tarragon, chives or parsley.

dover sole with a steak garnish

serves **two**

1 tablespoon finely
  chopped shallots
  or onion
2 tablespoons
  white wine vinegar
salt and pepper
125g (4½oz) softened
  butter
a squeeze of lemon
1 heaped teaspoon
  chopped tarragon
2 x 450–550g (1–1¼lb)
  Dover soles, skinned
2 plum tomatoes, halved
coarse sea salt
olive oil, for cooking
100g (4oz) button
  mushrooms
2 sprigs of watercress

Meaty Dover sole easily copes with this steak garnish of grilled tomatoes, mushrooms and watercress. The traditional Béarnaise sauce has been changed to a butter, binding together all the flavours, but a lot easier to make. The quantities are quite generous and any leftovers can be frozen.

- To make the Béarnaise butter, place the shallots, vinegar and a twist of pepper in a small saucepan. Allow to simmer until almost dry. Leave to cool. Mix the softened shallots with 100g (4oz) of the butter, adding the lemon juice and tarragon and seasoning with a pinch of salt.

- Preheat the grill. Place the soles on a greased baking tray along with the tomato halves. Brush with the remaining butter, saving a small knob for the mushrooms, and season with the coarse sea salt and pepper. Place the tray under the grill and cook for 8–10 minutes until a rich golden brown and cooked through. The soles need not be turned because the heat within the tray will cook them underneath.

- While grilling the fish, heat a frying pan with the olive oil and add the mushrooms and remaining knob of butter. Fry over a medium heat for a few minutes, turning them from time to time, until well coloured and tender.

- Place the soles on large plates, garnishing with the grilled tomatoes, fried mushrooms and watercress. Finish with a spoonful of Béarnaise butter on top.

salmon with a salted tomato and herb salad

serves **four** as a starter

16–20 cherry tomatoes
coarse sea salt and pepper
4 tablespoons extra-virgin
  olive oil, plus a trickle
  for cooking
1 tablespoon lime juice
1 tablespoon chopped
  mixed herbs (tarragon,
  chervil, basil, chives,
  coriander)
4 x 100g (4oz) salmon
  fillets, skinned
15g (½oz) butter

This recipe is a starter, but adding a green salad and warm new potatoes would make it a main course. The selection of herbs also doesn't have to be as great as I've chosen.

• Halve the tomatoes horizontally, seasoning the cut sides with a generous sprinkling of sea salt and a twist of pepper.

• Whisk together the olive oil, lime juice and herbs, seasoning with salt and pepper.

• Pat the salmon dry on kitchen paper. Trickle a little oil into a non-stick frying pan over a medium heat. Add the butter, and once bubbling, put in the fish. Cook gently for 3–4 minutes before turning the fillets and removing the pan from the heat. The residual heat in the pan will continue to cook the fish for a further minute or so.

• While the salmon is resting, divide the tomatoes among the plates, spooning over the herb dressing. Place the salmon beside the tomatoes to serve.

whole poached salmon with a cucumber salad

serves **four–six**

1.5kg (3lb 5oz)
  whole salmon
300ml (10fl oz) white wine
1 teaspoon caster sugar
1 tablespoon lime juice
4 tablespoons olive oil
a splash of white
  wine vinegar
salt and pepper
1 large cucumber,
  peeled and sliced

This dish makes a fabulous starter, but is also a simple way of feeding lots of people at a party. I've just sliced the cucumber for this dish, but you could replace it with cucumber pappardelle (see page 355).

- Put the salmon in a fish kettle or suitable sized pan, add the wine and top up with cold water until covered. Cover, bring gently to a simmer and cook for 6–8 minutes. Remove from the heat and leave to cool with the lid on until just warm.

- While the salmon is cooling, warm the sugar and lime juice in a small saucepan to dissolve the sugar. Remove from the heat, whisk in the oil and vinegar and season with salt and pepper.

- Once the salmon is at room temperature, drizzle the lime dressing through the cucumber and season with a pinch of salt and pepper.

- Lift the salmon from the pan and present whole at the table, the flesh flaking away easily for everybody to help themselves. Alternatively, portions can be spooned from the bone on to the plates and served with the cucumber salad.

and more

The skin of the salmon can easily be pulled away to remove before serving.

A heaped teaspoon of chopped dill or chives can be added to the dressing.

To enrich the cooking liquid, a fish stock cube can be sprinkled into the pan along with a few peppercorns, a star anise, bay leaf and some herbs such as tarragon or parsley.

Likewise, the liquor can be enhanced by the addition of some thinly sliced vegetables: a couple of carrots, an onion, some celery and a small bulb of fennel.

steamed salmon with grilled vegetables

serves **four**

8 asparagus spears
2 small–medium
  courgettes
2 red peppers
1 small aubergine
1 red onion
2 teaspoons
  red wine vinegar
1 tablespoon orange juice
a pinch of sugar
2 tablespoons olive oil,
  plus extra for drizzling
coarse sea salt and pepper
4 x 175g (6oz) salmon
  fillets, skinned
a large knob of butter

I love this contrast of flavours: tender, steamed salmon with vibrant, smoky vegetables. By the way, the vegetables can be purely your choice. Below I've listed some of my favourites.

- Snap the woody end from each asparagus spear and split the courgettes in half lengthways. Quarter the peppers, removing the seeds. Slice the aubergine into four lengthways and cut the red onion into four thick circles.

- Whisk the red wine vinegar, orange juice and sugar together. Add the olive oil and season with salt and pepper.

- Lightly toss all of the vegetables in a drizzle of olive oil. Preheat a ridged griddle pan and grill the vegetables for 3–5 minutes on each side until they have reached a deep, grill-marked brown and are tender. Once cooked, put the vegetables into a large bowl, season with a pinch of sea salt and drizzle with the dressing.

- While grilling the vegetables, smear the salmon with the butter and sprinkle a little sea salt on top. Place in a steamer and steam for 6–8 minutes over rapidly simmering water before serving with the grilled vegetables.

and more

A large spoonful of mayonnaise or thick crème fraîche on the side, perhaps mixed with chopped herbs, is very tasty.

roast sea bass and potatoes with a shrimp cream

serves **four**

4 baking potatoes
100ml (3½fl oz) olive oil
coarse sea salt and pepper
1.5kg (3lb 5oz)
  whole sea bass
25g (1oz) melted butter
1 heaped tablespoon finely
  chopped shallots or onion
1 glass of white wine
150ml (5fl oz)
  chicken stock
150ml (5fl oz) double cream
100g (4oz) cooked and
  peeled shrimps or
  small prawns
1 teaspoon
  chopped tarragon
a squeeze of lemon

- Preheat the oven to 220°C/425°F/gas 7. Cut each of the potatoes lengthways into three slices and mix with the olive oil in a bowl. Arrange the slices in a large roasting tray. Sprinkle with sea salt and pepper and roast for 25 minutes.

- Brush the sea bass, inside and out, with the butter and season with sea salt and pepper. After 25 minutes of roasting the potatoes, place the sea bass on top and return the tray to the oven. Continue to roast for a further 25 minutes until the sea bass and potatoes are cooked.

- While roasting the bass, boil together the shallots and white wine in a small saucepan until almost dry. Pour in the stock and cream and simmer to a loose sauce consistency. Just before serving, add the shrimps, tarragon and lemon juice and season with salt and pepper if needed

- Place a few roast potato slices on each plate, then spoon the flesh from the backbone of the sea bass and arrange on top, pouring over the sauce.

and more

A green salad tossed with lemon and olive oil is a great alternative to the shrimp cream.

toasted sea bass and oranges with basil yoghurt

serves **four**

3 large oranges
150ml (5fl oz)
  natural yoghurt
1 large bunch or a small
  pot of basil
salt
4 x 175g (6oz) sea bass
  fillets, skin on
olive oil, for brushing
coarse sea salt
demerara sugar,
  for sprinkling

The skin of the sea bass can be scored by cutting across it for an attractively crispy result.

• To segment the oranges, top and tail the fruits using a serrated edged knife. The rind and pith can now be removed by cutting in a sawing motion down the sides. To release the segments, simply cut between each membrane and place the segments on a baking tray.

• Pour the yoghurt into a food processor or blender with the basil leaves. Blend until smooth, seasoning with a pinch of salt. If the sauce is too thick, water can be added to loosen it.

• Preheat the oven grill. Grease a baking tray and arrange the sea bass fillets on top, skin-side up. Brush each with olive oil and season with a sprinkling of sea salt before placing under the grill, as close to the top as possible. Grill for just 2–3 minutes until golden brown and crispy, then move the tray to a lower shelf.

• Sprinkle the orange segments with the demerara sugar and place them under the grill. These will need just a minute to warm through, while the warmth also completes the cooking of the fish below. The sea bass, oranges and basil sauce are now ready to serve.

sea bass with leek carbonara

serves **four**

4 x 175g (6oz) sea bass
 fillets, skin on
salt and pepper
flour, for dusting
olive oil, for cooking
2 large knobs of butter
6 rashers of streaky
 bacon, cut into thin strips
3 leeks, cut into
 thick slices
150ml (5fl oz) double or
 whipping cream
2 generous tablespoons
 grated Parmesan cheese

Eggs are omitted from this carbonara recipe and just cream used to bind the bacon, Parmesan and leeks.

• Dry the sea bass on kitchen paper, season with salt and pepper and lightly dust the skin with flour. Heat the olive oil in a non-stick frying pan and add a large knob of butter. Once it begins to sizzle, place the fish in the pan skin-side down. The fish may need to be gently pressed down with a fish slice because the skin tightens in the heat, slightly curving the fillets. The sea bass will take 6–7 minutes to crisp and colour before turning it and removing from the heat. The residual warmth in the pan will continue the cooking process.

• While the fish is frying, heat a large saucepan on top of the stove and add the bacon. Fry for a few minutes until golden, then spoon the strips on to a plate and pour away the excess fat in the pan. Add the remaining butter and, once melted, stir in the leeks along with 3 tablespoons of water. Cover and allow the leeks to steam for a few minutes until tender.

• Pour the cream over, simmering until lightly thickened, then spoon the Parmesan cheese and bacon through the sauce. The leeks are now ready to serve with the sea bass on top.

and more

Salmon, cod, turbot, tuna and John Dory will all very comfortably substitute for the sea bass.

The leeks can also be cut into long strips resembling tagliatelle.

skate with sizzling tartare butter

serves **four**

4 x 225g (8oz) skate
  wings, skinned
salt and pepper
flour, for dusting
olive oil, for cooking
100g (4oz) butter
1 tablespoon capers
1 tablespoon chopped
  gherkins
1 tablespoon finely
  chopped shallots
  or onion
1 tablespoon
  chopped parsley
juice of 1 lemon

- Preheat the oven to 200°C/400°F/gas 6. Pat the skate wings dry on kitchen paper, season with salt and pepper and dust lightly with flour. Heat the olive oil in a large non-stick ovenproof frying pan or roasting tray on top of the stove. Once hot, place the wings in the pan, frying for a few minutes until golden brown. Turn the wings over, leaving them in the pan for a further 1–2 minutes before placing the pan in the oven and roasting for 8–10 minutes. Once cooked, carefully lift the wings on to plates.

- Melt the butter in the frying pan until it is just beginning to foam and reach a nutty brown stage. Add the capers, gherkins, shallots and parsley, squeezing the lemon juice over. Once the tartare butter begins to sizzle, spoon over the skate wings to serve.

warm skate and bacon salad

serves **four**

4 x 175–225g (6–8oz) skate
  wings, filleted and skinned
salt and pepper
1 large lemon
8 rashers of smoked
  streaky bacon
1 tablespoon red wine
  vinegar
1 teaspoon Dijon or
  wholegrain mustard
3 tablespoons walnut or
  groundnut oil
1 round lettuce
2 Little Gem lettuces
1–2 tablespoons low-fat
  crème fraîche (optional)

Skate wings are generally sold skinned. Here they are also filleted, which your fishmonger should be happy to do for you.

• Cut each skate fillet into two or three strips. Season with salt and pepper and squeeze lemon juice all over them. Roughly chop the squeezed lemon, adding it to the water for steaming the fish.

• Cut the bacon into pieces the width of your thumb. Heat a frying pan and once hot, scatter in the bacon, frying quickly until golden brown. Remove the bacon from the pan, reserving the bacon fat, and keep warm.

• Whisk the red wine vinegar and mustard into the saved bacon fat, adding the oil and seasoning with salt and pepper.

• Place the lemon skate in a steamer and steam for 5–8 minutes over rapidly simmering water until tender to the touch. While steaming, tear the salad leaves into a bowl, mixing with the warm bacon and the dressing. Add the skate to the salad and drizzle over the crème fraîche, if using.

lemon fish fingers with an avocado and lime dip

serves **four**

1 ripe avocado,
 roughly chopped
juice of 1 lime
100ml (3½fl oz)
 mayonnaise
a few drops of Tabasco
salt and pepper
550g (1¼lb) lemon sole
 fillets, skinned
flour, for dusting
2 beaten eggs
100g (4oz) fresh white
 breadcrumbs
oil, for deep-frying

- Put the avocado into a food processor with the lime juice and mayonnaise. Season with a few drops of Tabasco and a pinch of salt and blitz until smooth. Refrigerate the dip until ready to serve.

- Cut the lemon sole into strips about the length and width of your little finger and season with salt and pepper. Lightly dust a handful at a time in flour, then coat in the egg and breadcrumbs. Continue with the remainder, keeping the fish fingers separate to prevent them from becoming soggy.

- Heat the oil in a large pan or deep-fat fryer to 180–190°C (350–375°F) and fry a handful of fish fingers for 1–2 minutes until crispy golden brown. Using a slotted spoon, lift the fish fingers from the oil on to a kitchen-paper-lined plate or tray. Once the oil is back to the correct temperature, continue to fry the remainder.

- Stack a plate or bowl with the fish fingers and serve with the avocado and lime dip.

and more

Plaice, dab or flounder can be used instead of the lemon sole.

For a real lemon bite, add the finely grated zest of a lemon to the breadcrumbs.

trout salad with ham and a yoghurt piccalilli

serves **four** as a starter

2 heaped tablespoons
  piccalilli
2–3 tablespoons natural
  yoghurt
4 trout fillets, skin on
1 round lettuce
4 thin slices of ham
coarse sea salt
olive oil, for drizzling

Skinned trout fillets can be used in this recipe, but I prefer to wait until the fish have been steamed, when the skins can be pulled away easily.

- Spoon the piccalilli and 2 tablespoons of the yoghurt into a food processor or blender. Blitz until smooth, adding the remaining tablespoon of yoghurt for a creamier taste.

- Put the trout fillets on a plate in a steamer and steam over rapidly simmering water for a few minutes until firm but still maintaining a slightly springy touch.

- While the trout is cooking, arrange the lettuce leaves among the plates. Lay the ham slices over the leaves and spoon the yoghurt piccalilli dressing over and around.

- Peel off the skin from the trout, laying each fillet on top of the salad. Sprinkle with a few sea salt flakes and drizzle with 1–2 drops of olive oil.

and more

The ham slices can be torn into bite-size pieces and strewn among the leaves.

Grilled mackerel fillets and quickly seared tuna both suit this salad very well.

trout with roasted hazelnut butter

serves **four**

25g (1oz) skinned
  hazelnuts, chopped
100g (4oz) softened
  butter, plus a large
  knob for brushing
2 tablespoons hazelnut oil
1 tablespoon
  tarragon vinegar
salt and pepper
8 trout fillets, skin on
1 tablespoon chopped
  chives

The hazelnut butter can be made in advance and refrigerated but make sure it is close to room temperature before serving. If you don't have any hazelnut oil, just replace with walnut or olive.

• Preheat the grill. Scatter the hazelnuts on to a baking tray and place under the grill, toasting to a rich golden brown to create the roasted flavour. Allow to cool before beating into the butter with the oil and vinegar. Season with salt and pepper.

• Grease a baking tray and place the fish on the tray, skin-side up. Brush the skin with the knob of butter and season with a pinch of salt. Place under the grill, toasting for just a few minutes until the trout begin to colour and crisp.

• Arrange the trout on plates, spooning the roasted hazelnut butter on top. Sprinkle with the chives and serve.

and more

These trout fillets taste wonderful with a crispy salad or warm spinach or courgettes.

ham-wrapped trout with an english mustard sauce

serves **four**

20–24 sage leaves
4 trout
salt and pepper
4 slices of Parma ham
olive oil, for cooking
1 teaspoon English
  mustard
½ teaspoon clear honey
1 tablespoon red wine
  vinegar
2 teaspoons mayonnaise
3 tablespoons walnut or
  groundnut oil
a large knob of butter

- Preheat the oven to 200°C/400°F/gas 6. Place 5–6 sage leaves inside each fish, seasoning with salt and pepper. Wrap a slice of Parma ham around the centre of the fish, brushing the trout liberally with some olive oil.

- Heat a baking tray on top of the stove and brush with olive oil. Once hot, place the trout on carefully, transferring the tray to the oven and roasting for 10 minutes until cooked through.

- While roasting the fish, whisk together the mustard, honey, vinegar and mayonnaise in a food processor or blender. Continue to whisk while drizzling the walnut or groundnut oil into the mix. The consistency should be just thin enough to pour without being runny. If it is too thick, loosen with 1–2 teaspoons of water. Season with a pinch of salt.

- Lift the trout on to the plates, returning the baking tray to the stove. Once hot, melt the knob of butter into the trout juices and spoon over the fish. Drizzle the sauce over or serve separately.

and more

Should English mustard be a little too fiery for your taste buds, replace with wholegrain or Dijon mustard.

cod with melting gruyère, spinach and mushrooms

serves **four**

4 x 175g (6oz)
  cod fillets, skinned
salt and pepper
flour, for dusting
olive oil, for cooking
50g (2oz) butter
225g (8oz) chestnut
  mushrooms, sliced
400g (14oz) baby spinach
100g (4oz) grated
  Gruyère cheese
6 tablespoons
  double cream

Chestnut mushrooms have a slightly nutty bite, which partners the spinach very well. During the autumn months, wild mushrooms make a wonderful alternative.

• Preheat the oven to 200°C/400°F/gas 6. Dry the cod fillets, season with salt and pepper and lightly dust each in flour. Heat the olive oil in a non-stick ovenproof frying pan on top of the stove. Once hot, fry the fillets, skinned-side down, for several minutes until golden brown. Turn them over and transfer the pan to the oven, roasting for 6–8 minutes and basting from time to time to help maintain the moistness of the fish.

• While roasting the cod, melt half the butter in a large pan and fry the mushrooms for 1–2 minutes until tender. Add the spinach leaves, season with salt and pepper and stir until the leaves begin to wilt.

• Preheat the grill. Mix the cheese with the double cream and spoon it on top of the cod fillets. Place under the grill until the cheese colours to a golden brown, softening and melting.

• Spoon the spinach and mushrooms on to the plates, whisking the remaining butter into any juices left in the pan. Trickle the butter over the spinach, placing the roasted cod on top.

and more

Haddock or coley can also be used, adjusting the cooking time to match the thickness of the fillets.

cod poached in a tarragon broth

serves **four**

2 carrots, thinly sliced
1 onion, sliced into rings
2 sticks of celery,
  thinly sliced
1 small leek, thinly sliced
1 bay leaf
1 sprig of thyme
a few black peppercorns
salt and pepper
150ml (5fl oz) orange juice
4 x 175g (6oz)
  cod fillets, skinned
a generous squeeze
  of lemon
1 teaspoon
  chopped tarragon

The tarragon broth in this recipe is similar to a court bouillon, an aromatic vegetable stock used for cooking fish. Here the cod and vegetables are cooked together in the broth to create the complete dish.

• Put the vegetables, bay leaf, thyme, peppercorns and a pinch of salt into a saucepan with enough space to hold the cod fillets. Cover with 300ml (10fl oz) water and allow to simmer for a few minutes until the vegetables are tender. Add the orange juice, boiling until just half the liquid is left.

• Season the cod with salt and pepper and place on top of the vegetables. Cover the pan and simmer gently for 8–10 minutes until the fish is firm to the touch and cooked through.

• Lift the fillets on to large plates or bowls. Add the lemon juice and tarragon to the broth, taste for seasoning and spoon with the vegetables over and around the cod.

and more

A wedge of butter stirred into the finished broth will give it a more saucy consistency.

cod with peas and ham stewed in butter

serves **four**

4 x 175g (6oz) cod fillets,
  skin on
salt and pepper
flour, for dusting
oil, for cooking
50g (2oz) butter, plus a
  knob for frying
450g (1lb) frozen peas
175g (6oz) piece of ham,
  cut into cubes
4 wedges of lemon

You'll notice frozen peas are listed in the ingredients to allow this recipe to be enjoyed throughout the year. However, between late spring and the early days of autumn, wonderful fresh peas will also be around.

• Pat the cod dry with kitchen paper, season with salt and pepper and lightly dust with flour.

• Heat some oil in a non-stick frying pan, place the fillets in the pan, skin-side down, and fry for 6–7 minutes until golden brown and crispy. Turn the fish in the pan, adding the knob of butter and cooking for a further minute.

• While frying the fish, cook the peas in a saucepan of boiling salted water until tender, then drain away the majority of the water, leaving around 100ml (3½fl oz). Add the ham, warming it through before seasoning with salt and pepper. Stir in the remaining butter.

• The crispy cod and peas are now ready to serve with a wedge of lemon.

and more

A little pinch of a chicken stock cube or an extra knob of butter can be stirred into the peas to enrich their flavour.

Mashed potatoes mixed with buttery spring onions make the perfect accompaniment.

grilled tuna with a niçoise salsa

serves **four**

4 large new potatoes
50g (2oz) fine French
  beans
2 spring onions
3 plum tomatoes,
  deseeded
1 small yellow pepper
4 anchovy fillets
8 stoned black olives
2 eggs
½ clove of garlic, crushed
½ tablespoon chopped
  chives
½ tablespoon chopped
  chervil
3 tablespoons olive oil,
  plus extra for brushing
salt and pepper
4 x 150g (5oz) tuna steaks

A ridged griddle pan is ideal for cooking the tuna here, those bitter, burnt lines adding earthiness to the dish. However it isn't essential; a frying pan will do.

- Cook the potatoes in boiling salted water for approximately 20 minutes until cooked through. When they have cooled down, peel them. Cook the French beans in boiling salted water until tender, but still with a bite. Quickly drain, running them under cold water to stop the cooking.

- Cut the beans, potatoes, spring onions, tomatoes, yellow pepper, anchovy fillets and olives into small pieces.

- Put the eggs into a pan of cold water, bring them to the boil and cook for 3 minutes before running under cold water until completely chilled. The eggs can now be shelled and chopped. Mix the eggs with the garlic, herbs and olive oil and season with salt and a twist of pepper. In a large bowl, spoon this dressing over the vegetables, mixing them all together.

- Preheat the griddle pan until hot. Brush the tuna steaks with olive oil, season with salt and a twist of pepper and lay on the hot griddle pan. Grill for 1–2 minutes on each side before serving with a spoonful or two of Niçoise salsa.

and more

Mix or drizzle a little low-fat crème fraîche over the salsa for a creamier flavour.

glazed horseradish tuna with hot spring onion potatoes

serves **four**

675g (1½lb) new potatoes
150ml (5fl oz) olive oil
3 teaspoons lemon juice
salt and pepper
2 slices of crustless bread,
  soaked in water
1 teaspoon
  white wine vinegar
2 egg yolks
2 tablespoons
  horseradish cream
1 tablespoon
  chopped chives
4 x 150g (5oz) tuna steaks
1 bunch of spring onions,
  thinly sliced

This horseradish glaze is quite fiery, but the quantity of horseradish cream can be reduced, or increased. Marinated in lemon oil, the hot new potatoes are delicious with this dish, but can be simply rolled in butter instead.

• Cook the new potatoes in boiling salted water for approximately 20 minutes until cooked through. Once cooked, drain and halve the potatoes into a bowl. Whisk together 4 tablespoons of the olive oil and the lemon juice, seasoning with salt and pepper. Pour the dressing over the potatoes and mix together well. Cover with clingfilm and keep warm to one side.

• Squeeze any excess water from the soaked bread and place it in a small bowl or blender with the vinegar and egg yolks. Using an electric hand whisk or the blender, blitz until smooth, slowly pouring in all but a tablespoon of the olive oil, a little at a time, as you would when making mayonnaise. Once mixed in, fold in the horseradish cream and chives and season with salt and pepper.

• Preheat the grill. Warm an ovenproof frying pan with the remaining olive oil and dry the tuna steaks on kitchen paper. Once hot, fry the tuna steaks for 1–2 minutes on each side before spooning the horseradish cream over generously. Pop the tuna under the grill, glazing to a golden brown.

• Stir the spring onions into the potatoes and serve with the tuna.

and more

A few salad leaves or sprigs of watercress are the perfect accompaniment to help mop up the horseradish glaze.

A spoonful of fresh peas or broad beans will complete the dish.

seared tuna with pissaladière toasts

serves **four**

olive oil, for cooking
a knob of butter
4 large onions,
  thinly sliced
1 clove of garlic,
  finely chopped
8 anchovy fillets, chopped
8 stoned black olives,
  chopped
salt and pepper
4 thick slices of country
  loaf or ciabatta
4 x 150g (5oz) tuna steaks

Pissaladière is an open, pizza-type onion tart from the south of France, flavoured with anchovies and black olives. The bread dough base is replaced here with simple toast.

- Heat 2 tablespoons of the olive oil and the butter together in a large frying pan. Add the onion and garlic and fry over a medium heat until tender and golden brown. Stir in the anchovies and olives, seasoning with salt and pepper.

- Toast the sliced bread. Heat some more olive oil in a non-stick frying pan. Pat the tuna dry with kitchen paper, season with salt and pepper, then place the steaks in the pan and sear for 2–3 minutes on each side.

- To serve, top each piece of toast with the pissaladière onions and a tuna steak.

and more

Mackerel is a good alternative fish to use in this dish.

Fresh herbs can also be added to the onions, thyme working particularly well, while tomatoes, peppers and other 'pizza topping' ingredients can become part of the pissaladière.

mackerel steamed with slivers of fennel

serves **four** as a starter

4 mackerel fillets
2 fennel bulbs
1 tablespoon lemon juice
4 spring onions, sliced
a pinch of caster sugar
coarse sea salt and pepper
melted butter, for brushing
1 teaspoon chopped
  fennel leaves or dill
3 tablespoons walnut oil

The mackerel fillets can be left whole or flaked into large pieces, mingling among the warm fennel.

- Take your mackerel fillets and if the fine bones haven't been removed, simply pull them out with tweezers.

- Using a mandolin, shred the fennel into paper-thin slices and put into a bowl. Add the lemon juice, spring onions and caster sugar and season with a sprinkling of coarse sea salt and a twist of pepper. Brush a sheet of foil with butter, arranging it in a steamer before scattering over the fennel mix.

- Place the mackerel fillets on top of the fennel, brushing each lightly with butter, and twist around the foil edges to save any juices released. Steam over rapidly simmering water for several minutes until the mackerel fillets are firm but still maintain a slightly springy touch.

- Remove the fish from the steamer, spooning the fennel and juices into a bowl. Stir in the fennel leaves and walnut oil, then divide the fennel among the plates or bowls and serve with the steamed mackerel.

and more

A couple of teaspoons of Pernod or one or two star anise can be added to enhance the aniseed flavour.

grilled mackerel with a caesar potato salad

serves **four** as a starter

4 mackerel fillets
350g (12oz) new potatoes
salt and pepper
150ml (5fl oz) mayonnaise
2 tablespoons lemon juice
1 small clove of
 garlic, crushed
1 teaspoon Dijon mustard
3 anchovy fillets
1 heaped teaspoon capers
a dash of Worcester sauce
2 tablespoons grated
 Parmesan cheese
melted butter, for brushing
half a small iceberg
 lettuce, torn into pieces

- Take your mackerel fillets and if the fine bones haven't been removed, simply pull them out with tweezers.

- Cook the new potatoes in boiling salted water for approximately 20 minutes until cooked through. Slice and season with salt and pepper, then keep warm to one side.

- Put the mayonnaise, lemon juice, garlic, mustard, anchovies, capers and Worcester sauce into a food processor or blender and blitz until smooth. If too thick, loosen with 1–2 teaspoons of water.

- Sprinkle the Parmesan cheese among the sliced potatoes, adding enough Caesar dressing to coat.

- Preheat the grill. Put the mackerel fillets on to a greased baking tray, brushing each with some butter and topping with a pinch of salt and some pepper. Cook under the grill for 3–4 minutes. Arrange the mackerel, Caesar potato salad and crispy iceberg on plates and serve immediately.

roast mackerel with smoked mackerel mash

serves **four**

4 x 350g (12oz) mackerel
coarse sea salt and pepper
olive oil, for cooking
a large knob of butter,
  plus extra for brushing
1 bunch of
  spring onions, sliced
2 smoked mackerel fillets,
  broken into flakes
1 x mash (see page 250)
1–2 tablespoons
  horseradish cream
4 wedges of lemon

- Preheat the oven to its highest temperature. Make three diagonal cuts in each side of the mackerels, cutting through to the bone. Season with salt and a twist of pepper and brush each with butter. Heat a roasting tray on top of the stove with the olive oil, carefully placing the fish in it. Transfer the tray to the oven and roast for 8–10 minutes.

- While roasting the mackerel, melt the knob of butter in a saucepan. Add the spring onions and cook them over a medium heat for 1–2 minutes until just beginning to soften. Sprinkle in the mackerel flakes, stirring to warm through before adding to the hot mash along with the horseradish cream.

- Serve the roast mackerel and mashed potatoes with a wedge of lemon.

and more

The horseradish cream can be replaced by English or Dijon mustard, adding a teaspoon at a time until your preferred strength is reached.

john dory with red pepper, tomato and basil spaghetti

serves **four**

4 tomatoes, quartered
100ml (3½fl oz) olive oil,
  plus extra for cooking
salt and pepper
1 clove of garlic, crushed
3 tablespoons tomato juice
1 tablespoon
  red wine vinegar
350g (12oz) spaghetti
2 large red peppers, cut
  into cubes
1 large red onion, chopped
8 basil leaves, chopped
4 x 150–175g (5–6oz)
  John Dory fillets, skin on
melted butter, for brushing

I quite often enjoy this spaghetti as a supper on its own, but the sweet flavour is enhanced by the grilled fish, which adds a bitter edge.

- Preheat the grill. Put the tomato quarters on to a baking tray, drizzling with olive oil and seasoning with salt and pepper. Place under the grill and cook for several minutes until softened and just beginning to colour. Once tender, spoon them into a blender and add the garlic, tomato juice and vinegar. Blitz until smooth before slowly pouring in the olive oil and mixing together.

- Cook the spaghetti until tender. While cooking the pasta, warm 2 tablespoons of the olive oil in a large deep frying pan or braising pan. Once hot, add the peppers and red onion, frying until coloured and tender. Drain the pasta and mix it in well with the tomato dressing, basil, peppers and red onion.

- Meanwhile, season the John Dory fillets with salt and pepper and lay on a greased baking tray, skin-side up, brushing with butter. Place under the hot grill, leaving for 4–5 minutes until the skin begins to colour and the fish is firmer but still tender to the touch. The John Dory and spaghetti are now ready to be served together on plates or in bowls.

and more

Mackerel, sea bass and tuna can also be used.

The tomato dressing can be strained through a sieve for a smoother finish and Parmesan finely grated over the spaghetti.

john dory with sautéed honey sesame courgettes

serves **four**

1 heaped tablespoon
  sesame seeds
4 tablespoons sour cream
2 teaspoons clear honey
salt and pepper
olive oil, for cooking
25g (1oz) butter, plus a
  knob for cooking
675g (1½lb)
  courgettes, sliced
4 x 150–175g (5–6oz)
  John Dory fillets, skinned
flour, for dusting

- Place the sesame seeds in a hot dry frying pan and toast for 1–2 minutes, shaking from time to time, until golden brown. Mix together the sour cream and honey, seasoning with salt and pepper. Heat some olive oil and the butter in a large saucepan and add the courgettes. Season with salt and pepper and fry for 5–6 minutes until golden brown and tender (thicker slices may need 1–2 extra minutes). Stir in the toasted sesame seeds.

- While cooking the courgettes, dry the John Dory on kitchen paper and season with salt and pepper before lightly flouring.

- Heat some more olive oil and the knob of butter in a non-stick frying pan and add the fish. Fry for 4–5 minutes until golden brown before turning and removing from the heat. The residual heat in the pan will continue the cooking.

- Spoon the honey sour cream over the courgettes, mixing it in well before dividing among the plates. Place the pan-fried John Dory on top or beside the courgettes and serve.

and more

This dish can also be made with turbot, cod, monkfish, sea bass or tuna.

Fresh chopped herbs, shallot rings and halved cherry tomatoes all work very well mixed in with the courgettes.

spicy monkfish bites with a cucumber and mint raita

serves **four**

300ml (10fl oz)
  natural yoghurt
juice of 2 limes
½ teaspoon turmeric
½ teaspoon paprika
¼ teaspoon ground
  cardamom
2 small cloves of
  garlic, crushed
salt and pepper
550g (1¼lb) monkfish
  fillets, cut into
  bite-sized pieces
1 cucumber
1 heaped teaspoon
  chopped mint
oil, for cooking

- In a large bowl, mix together 4 tablespoons of the yoghurt, the juice of 1 lime, the turmeric, paprika, cardamom, garlic and a pinch of salt. Add the monkfish pieces, stirring so they become totally covered.

- Peel and split the cucumber lengthways, scraping out the watery seeds before slicing. Mix together the remaining yoghurt, lime juice and mint, seasoning with salt and pepper. The cucumber slices can now be added to the mint yoghurt.

- Heat a wok or large frying pan with the oil. As the oil begins to smoke, carefully add the monkfish evenly around the pan. Fry for 4–5 minutes over a fast heat until the yoghurt has set around the monkfish pieces. Divide among the plates, offering the cucumber and mint raita separately.

melting mozzarella monkfish steaks with tomato and basil

serves **four**

5–6 tablespoons olive oil
1 clove of garlic, crushed
½ teaspoon honey
6 large, ripe plum
 tomatoes, deseeded and
 cut into small cubes
salt and pepper
8 x 50–75g (2–3oz)
 monkfish fillet steaks
flour, for dusting
2 buffalo mozzarella
1 tablespoon
 chopped basil

- To make the sauce, gently simmer 3 tablespoons of the olive oil and the garlic together in a small saucepan for a minute or two before stirring in the honey. Add the tomatoes and heat gently until they are just warm and softening. Season with salt and pepper and keep to one side.

- Pat dry the monkfish with kitchen paper and season with salt and pepper, lightly coating each piece in flour. Heat the remaining olive oil in a large non-stick frying pan and, once hot, place the monkfish in the pan. Fry for 2–3 minutes on each side, then transfer the steaks on to a baking tray.

- Preheat the grill. Slice the two mozzarellas into quarters and sit a slice on top of each monkfish steak. Pop the fish under the grill and leave until the mozzarella softens and begins to melt over the steaks.

- Add the basil to the warm tomato sauce, spooning it into large bowls or plates along with the mozzarella monkfish steaks.

turbot with mussel soup

serves **four**

675g (1½lb) mussels
1 glass of dry white wine
1 small fennel bulb
75g (3oz) butter
1 onion, finely chopped
2 sticks of celery,
  thinly sliced
1 small leek, thinly sliced
4 x 150–175g (5–6oz)
  turbot fillets, skinned
salt and pepper
1 tablespoon chopped
  parsley

This soupy version of *moules marinières*, combined here with turbot, needs plenty of bread to mop up the juices.

- Clean the mussels by washing them under cold running water, scraping away any barnacles and pulling out the beards that protrude from between the closed shells. If any mussels are found slightly open, a short, sharp tap should make them close, letting you know they are still alive. Any that don't close should be discarded.

- Put the mussels into a large saucepan with the white wine and 150ml (5fl oz) water. Cover with a lid and cook over a high heat for 3–7 minutes, shaking the pan and stirring the mussels from time to time until they have opened. Strain in a colander, saving all the cooking juices except the last couple of tablespoons, which tend to be gritty. Remove the cooked mussels from their shells, discarding any that have not opened.

- Quarter the fennel, cutting away the core before shredding finely. Melt 25g (1oz) of the butter in a saucepan, add the fennel, onion, celery and leek and cook gently for a few minutes before straining the mussel juices over the top. Simmer until the vegetables are tender, adding the mussels at the end to warm through.

- Season the turbot fillets with a pinch of salt and a twist of pepper and lay them, skinned-side up, on a plate and top with a square of parchment paper. Place the plate in a steamer and steam for 6–8 minutes over rapidly simmering water until just springy to the touch.

- Pour any turbot juices saved on the plate into the mussels and stir in the remaining butter and the parsley. Ladle the mussels into large bowls and place the turbot on top.

and more

The parsley can be mixed with tarragon and chervil for a more herby sauce.

turbot and creamy smoked salmon cabbage

serves **four**

½ green cabbage,
  cut into strips
1 heaped tablespoon
  finely chopped shallots
  or onion
1 glass of dry white wine
150ml (5fl oz)
  double cream
4 x 175g (6oz) turbot
  fillets, skinned
salt and pepper
flour, for dusting
oil, for cooking
a knob of butter
coarse sea salt
4 slices of smoked
  salmon, cut into strips

- Cook the cabbage in a large saucepan of boiling salted water for a few minutes until tender, then drain.

- Put the shallots and white wine into a saucepan and boil until just a quarter of the liquid is left. Pour in the cream and return to a simmer before adding the cooked cabbage and heating through.

- Meanwhile, pat the turbot dry on kitchen paper, season with salt and pepper and lightly dust with flour. Heat the oil in a non-stick frying pan and, once hot, lay the turbot in the pan. Fry over a medium heat for 5–6 minutes to a light golden brown before adding the knob of butter. Turn the fillets and remove the pan from the heat. Sprinkle a few flakes of sea salt on top of each.

- Spoon the strips of smoked salmon into the cabbage, season with a twist of pepper if needed and divide the creamy cabbage among the plates. Serve with the pan-fried turbot, spooning any remaining butter in the frying pan over the fish.

and more

This cabbage works equally well with halibut, brill, salmon or sea bass.

A squeeze of lemon juice can be added, which complements the creamy smoked salmon.

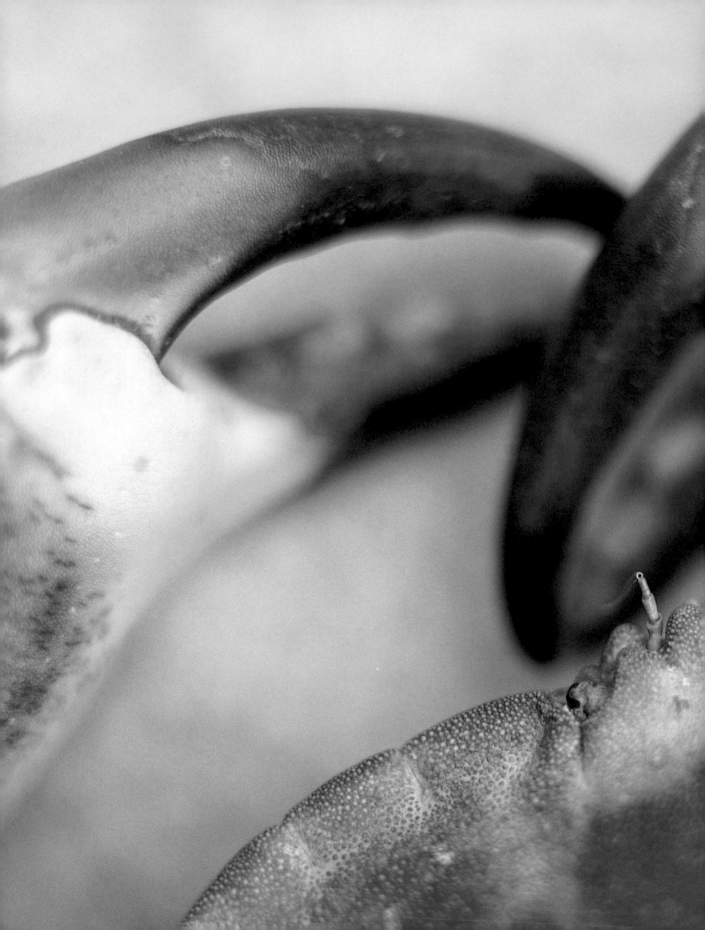

fish **seafood** poultry pork lamb beef vegetables pasta and rice eggs and cheese desserts

keeping seafood simple

Eating seafood is fun. Cracking open claws and peeling prawns makes your table come alive, everyone hunting down the sweet meat hidden inside the shells. And now that seafood can be bought all pre-prepared and ready to go, you can also bypass any aggravation and enjoy seafood that's easy to cook and eat. If you're thinking simple, the best thing is that you never need to overwork shellfish. The flavour is there to be enhanced, not masked.

how to choose seafood

Seafood is seasonal so look at what's available. If shellfish don't look at their best or are very small, they're probably coming out of season and won't be as affordable. However, these days seafood does come in all year round from warm waters, particularly prawns, so there is usually a decent choice.

Seafood is easily found frozen and this is a good option. Buy what you can and experiment.

Each kind of seafood has a distinctive taste, but a similar tone means that one of the best things about cooking with shellfish is that you can switch whatever you find or enjoy eating into any one of the recipes.

Prawns can be a wonderful stand-in if other seafood is too expensive or unavailable. Invest in tiger prawns and use instead of lobsters or langoustines.

If you're buying octopus or squid, buy the smallest you can find. These are the most tender and they need less preparation.

Freshness is very important when buying seafood. Most seafood will keep for 24 hours in your fridge if you've bought it nice and fresh, but really the fresher you eat it, the fuller the flavour. Even when buying precooked seafood, you should be able to smell the sea on it.

How much?

Mussels: 500g (1lb 2oz) mussels per person generally allows around 15–20 mussels each.

Scallops: Buy 4–5 large scallops per person for a main course.

Oysters: 5–6 oysters each makes for a generous starter.

Crab: A 1kg (2¼lb) whole crab will provide roughly 350g (12oz) crabmeat.

Lobster: For a whole lobster, you need roughly 450g (1lb) per person for a main course.

Prawns: The amount required really depends on size and what you need them for. The recipes will give you a good idea on quantities.

Langoustines: About 5–6 per person for a main course, depending on size.

Squid: 4–5 baby squid should be enough for each person.

a summer seafood platter

A cold seafood platter put together from ready-cooked shellfish creates a sensational centrepiece for a summer lunch for family or friends. Below are some favourites that you would definitely find on my table, along with plenty of napkins and bowls of iced water and lemon for cleaning up all the mess.

Crab. A lot of people will tell you that crab are better than lobster, and certainly one of the great things about them is that you can buy them totally pre-prepared and cooked, making it easy to get at the meat. Dressed crabs, where the crabmeat has even been taken out for you and packed back into the body, are also easily available. Whatever you buy, though, always do a quick second check with your fingertips to remove any splinters of shell.

To serve at their best: Crab makes a great pre-starter, just set on the table for everyone to pick at while you finish getting lunch ready.

Oysters. Always bought alive and trembling, there are usually two varieties available, the Pacific and the more flavoursome native, whose natural season is any month that contains the letter 'r'. I suggest you try the Pacific because, although it lacks the reputation of the native, it is available throughout the summer, still offers a good flavour and costs a lot less.

To serve at their best: Eat oysters raw in the French style with a bowl of sharp red wine vinegar and chopped shallots. And you don't have to swallow them whole, chewing them actually releases extra flavours.

Lobster. I think lobsters have an image of being quite frightening creatures for the cook to deal with, so I would suggest to anybody who is a bit afraid, not to start with the live ones, but buy a couple of cooked lobsters for a weekend starter.

To serve at their best: If you're sharing your lobsters with guests, turn them into an extravagant little starter by serving alongside a glass of dry white wine or champagne.

Prawns. North Atlantic prawns are the most common prawns found in the UK, but the larger king or tiger prawns are wonderful because as well as being available cooked, they can also be bought uncooked in the shell, ready to be popped straight on a griddle or barbecue, head, shell and all, for a few minutes. Peel to reveal their meaty texture, perfect for dunking in a garlic mayonnaise.

To serve at their best: Buy cooked prawns in their shells for a warm salad. Peel and add the shells to some tarragon and warm olive oil to make a hot salad dressing. Pour over the prawns and salad leaves with some lemon juice and seasoning.

hot seafood starters for winter

In the colder months when you want your seafood served piping hot, you can still keep it simple by buying it precooked, requiring only enough heat to warm through. Pick something from my choices below of some of the simplest seafood to cook.

Langoustines. The finest way to eat cooked or raw langoustines is to steam them in their shells in a trickle of water and put them straight on the table for everyone to pick at.

To serve at their best: Accompany with a pot of mayonnaise or a little horseradish cream.

Mussels. At their best in the winter months, you can now buy your mussels alive but cleaned, washed and ready to pop into a pan. Just cook with white wine, a splash of water, a knob of butter and a squeeze of lemon until all the mussels have opened.

To serve at their best: Turn the mussels out into a large bowl and enjoy with bread to mop up the juices.

Squid. This is ABC food. If you buy it already cleaned, it's as quick to prepare and cook as a fried egg. Cut the smallest baby squid into rings and fry in a little oil over a very high heat. This fast cooking gives you the tenderest result, but if you do overcook it, braise it in a little fish stock until it becomes tender again.

To serve at their best: Quickly stir-fry baby squid with cooked mangetout, toasted sesame seeds and sesame oil.

Scallops. If you can find them in their shells, ask your fishmonger to open and clean them for you ready to eat super-fresh the same day. Simply fry the sweet meat in butter for a minute or so on each side and squeeze over a little lemon juice. If you've bought them out of shell, dry them on kitchen paper and sear very quickly to save all the juices and give them a bitter edge that makes a lovely contrast to their soft texture.

To serve at their best: We tend to eat them at home pan-fried with a salad dressed with a splash of soy sauce, grated fresh ginger and spring onion.

key flavours for seafood

Lemon juice. If it's seafood, lemon (or lime) juice can partner everything.

Parma ham and bacon. These work surprisingly well with shellfish.

Pesto. Lovely as a dip or stirred into a side bowl of mayonnaise or hollandaise.

Green vegetables. Almost anything green seems to go with seafood. Spinach or fresh peas are natural partners for scallops, while soft, buttery leeks go perfectly with any shellfish.

Flavoured butters. Melt over a grilled lobster or prawns.

Tarragon and sorrel. These are beautiful herbs for seafood. Basil, chervil, dill and fennel tops are also marvellous, but thyme and oregano, if not used carefully, can be too overpowering.

Salad leaves. A green salad goes really well with cold or warm seafood.

Mango and papaya. Try either in a little salsa with grated fresh ginger and chilli.

simple seafood suppers

Pan-fried scallops with oniony mash. Quickly sear scallops and serve with mashed potatoes and a little sauce of onions very slowly cooked in butter and caramelized with some sugar.

Colcannon crab cakes. Mix cooked crab with Colcannon potato made from mash, cooked cabbage and cream, pat into little cakes and lightly pan-fry.

Squid with a walnut and orange salad. Make a salad from cracked walnuts, lettuce leaves, walnut oil and wedges of orange to serve with quickly pan-fried squid.

Prawns, tomato and fresh herb pasta. Make a quick after-work supper by cooking together some chopped onion, cooked prawns, passata and torn basil.

Warm oysters with hollandaise. Steam oysters in their shells for 4–5 minutes, opening them up to eat with a spoonful of hollandaise.

Crab Caesar salad. Add flakes of crab to a quick Caesar salad made from cos lettuce leaves, crispy bacon and Parmesan. Add extra lemon juice to the Caesar or mayonnaise dressing.

Quick-fried squid with herb and garlic butter. Pan-fry baby squid over a high heat and melt a spoonful of herb and garlic butter in the pan just before serving.

Gratinéed crab toasts. Top fingers of toast with crabmeat mixed with mayonnaise and cream and grill until just toasted.

Grilled oysters with a summer dressing. Grill or pan-fry shelled oysters for no more than a couple of minutes to warm through, then mix their juices into a salad dressing and pour over immediately to serve.

simple sauces for seafood

mayonnaise

makes **300ml** (10fl oz)

2 egg yolks
1 tablespoon
  white wine vinegar
1 heaped teaspoon
  English or Dijon mustard
300ml (10fl oz) groundnut
  or sunflower oil
salt and pepper
a squeeze of lemon

One of the most versatile sauces we know, this easy-to-make mayonnaise can accompany almost anything. These days there are also plenty of good-quality jars of mayonnaise available, so it's not essential to make your own.

• Place the egg yolks, vinegar and mustard in a blender or food processor and mix together. Very slowly, drop by drop, whisk in the oil. As the mayonnaise begins to thicken, create a thin stream of oil, continuing to pour until it has totally blended with the yolks.

• Season with salt and pepper and finish with the lemon juice.

• The mayonnaise is now ready to serve or can be kept refrigerated in a sealed jar or container for 2–3 days.

and more

Half the groundnut or sunflower oil can be replaced by olive oil, but not extra-virgin olive oil as this, I feel, is too strong. An equal quantity of groundnut or sunflower oil with olive oil is a well-balanced combination.

prawn rarebits

serves **four** as bites or
two as a starter

4–6 thick slices of
  French bread
melted butter, for brushing
1 teaspoon
  English mustard
a dash of Worcester sauce
150ml (5fl oz) double or
  whipping cream
75g (3oz) grated
  Cheddar cheese
75g (3oz) grated
  Gruyère cheese
175g (6oz) cooked and
  peeled prawns

This cheese sauce is instantly created with cream and can also be used to top chicken breasts, baked potatoes or even to make a quick lobster thermidor. Just replace the Worcester sauce with lemon juice, spoon over the cooked lobster and brown under the grill.

- Preheat the grill. Brush both sides of each bread slice with butter and toast the top and bottom to a golden brown under the grill.

- In a large bowl, stir the mustard and Worcester sauce into the cream. Extra mustard can be added for a stronger taste. Loosely fold in the cheese and prawns, then spoon the mixture on to the toasts.

- Place under the grill, not too close to the top, and toast to a golden brown. The rarebits are now ready to serve.

butterflied prawns with sweet and sour papaya

serves **four**

16 raw tiger or king
  prawns, peeled
melted butter, for brushing
coarse sea salt and pepper
2 ripe papayas
50g (2oz) fresh
  red chillies, deseeded
  and roughly chopped
1 teaspoon caster sugar
1–2 tablespoons white
  wine vinegar
1 clove of garlic,
  finely crushed
1 tablespoon
  Thai fish sauce
3 tablespoons clear honey
juice of 1 lime

• Using a sharp knife, make a deep incision along the back of the prawns, cutting virtually halfway through the meat to create a natural butterfly shape.

• Butter a baking tray, then lay the prawns on their sides on top. Brush each with butter and sprinkle with a little sea salt and pepper.

• Halve the papayas and cut each half into six wedges, peeling away the skin. Cut the wedges into cubes.

• Place the chillies in a food processor with all the remaining ingredients and blend until almost puréed and smooth. The sauce is now ready.

• Preheat the grill. Place the prawns under the grill and cook for 2 minutes until warm and tender.

• While grilling the prawns, stir the sauce into the papaya, then spoon the fruit into plates or bowls. The prawns can now be placed on top of the papaya to serve.

and more

Some chopped coriander leaves can be mixed in with the papaya.

tiger prawns with a leek and mozzarella risotto

serves **four**

12–16 raw tiger prawns, peeled
1 tablespoon olive oil, plus extra for drizzling
75g (3oz) butter, plus a large knob for brushing
1 large onion, chopped
1 leek, sliced
225g (8oz) arborio rice
1 glass of white wine
900ml (1½ pints) hot vegetable or chicken stock
salt and pepper
2 tablespoons grated mozzarella
2 tablespoons grated Parmesan cheese
1 heaped tablespoon chopped flat-leaf parsley (optional)

If tiger prawns are not available, a couple of handfuls of peeled prawns added to the risotto to warm through make for a tasty supper dish. The quantity of stock listed is quite generous and not all may be needed.

- Soak four bamboo skewers in cold water for 15 minutes. Dry the prawns on kitchen paper, then pierce 3–4 on to each bamboo skewer. Refrigerate until needed.

- Warm the olive oil and 25g (1oz) of the butter in a braising pan. Once bubbling, add the onion and leek, cooking for several minutes until soft and transparent. Add the rice, stirring the grains in the butter for 2 minutes until well coated. Pour in the white wine and cook until completely absorbed. Add a ladleful of hot stock and stir until also absorbed. Repeat this process, stirring continuously, for about 20 minutes until the rice is tender and creamy with a slight bite left in the centre. Season with salt and pepper and remove the pan from the heat. Add the mozzarella, Parmesan, parsley, if using, and remaining butter. Stir thoroughly, loosening with a little more stock if necessary, then cover with a lid and leave to rest.

- Preheat the grill. Drizzle a baking tray with olive oil, season the prawn skewers with salt and pepper and lay on the tray. Brush each skewer with the knob of butter and grill for 2 minutes before turning and cooking for a further couple of minutes.

- The risotto and prawns are now ready to serve. Arrange them together on plates or bowls, drizzling any butter and oil from the baking tray over the prawns.

crab claws with a dressed dip

serves **four** as a starter

3 eggs
100ml (3½fl oz) double
  or whipping cream
  or crème fraîche
4 generous
  tablespoons mayonnaise
1 heaped teaspoon
  chopped parsley
1 heaped teaspoon
  chopped capers
a squeeze of lemon
salt
a pinch of cayenne pepper
16–20 crab claws

Crab claws are generally sold frozen, cooked and ready to eat. The dressed dip binds together the ingredients normally associated with dressed crab to provide you with an easy starter.

• Put the eggs into boiling water, return to the boil and cook for 8 minutes. Place the pan under cold running water, leaving it to run until cold. Shell the eggs and roughly chop the white and yolks.

• In a small bowl, whisk the cream until lightly whipped. Add the mayonnaise, mixing it in well, then stir in the egg, parsley and capers with a generous squeeze of lemon juice. Season with a pinch of salt and cayenne pepper and spoon the dip into a suitable bowl. The claws and dip are now ready to eat.

and more

Arranging the claws with a green salad tossed with the dressed sauce creates a nice starter.

The claws can be pan-fried in butter and served warm with the dip.

crab dip with home-made crisps

serves **four** as a starter

2 medium potatoes,
  unpeeled
oil, for deep-frying
salt
100–150ml (3½–5fl oz)
  crème fraîche
1–2 teaspoons lemon juice
1 tablespoon olive oil
225g (8oz) white crabmeat
a pinch of cayenne pepper

This is a dish that can take on so many identities and be offered as savoury canapés, a starter or an elaborate salad. This version is a starter, the crab dip scooped up on home-made crisps.

- Slice the potatoes very thinly, using a sharp knife or mandolin. Rinse well in cold water to help remove the starch before drying with a kitchen cloth. Heat the oil in a large pan, just a few inches deep, to 190°C (375°F). Fry the potatoes in small batches until golden brown. Remove using a slotted spoon, transfer on to kitchen paper and sprinkle with a pinch of salt.

- Mix 100ml (3½fl oz) of the crème fraîche with a teaspoon of lemon juice and the olive oil. Add the crabmeat, stirring the cream through well. If it's too thick, stir in the remaining crème fraîche and lemon juice, then season with a pinch of salt and cayenne pepper.

- The crab dip and crisps are ready to serve. Offer around in separate bowls or arrange together on plates.

and more

The crisps could be replaced by cubes of avocado on cocktail sticks.

langoustines with a basil and mango sauce

serves **four**

1 very ripe large mango
100ml (3½fl oz) olive oil
2–4 teaspoons sherry
  vinegar
salt
a few basil leaves,
  chopped
20–24 langoustines,
  shell on

Also known as Dublin Bay prawns, these mini lobster lookalikes are just sensational to eat. The tails peel as you would prawns, which incidentally are also lovely with this sauce.

• Cut away the skin of the mango, chopping the flesh and placing it in a blender or food processor. Blitz to a purée, gradually trickling in the olive oil while the blender is still running. Add the sherry vinegar to taste and season with salt before stirring in the basil.

• Drop the langoustines into a steamer and steam over rapidly boiling water for just a few minutes, depending on the size of the langoustines. Serve with the basil and mango sauce.

grilled lobster with garlic and parsley butter

serves **four**

2 x 750g (1lb 10oz)
  cooked lobsters
4 cloves of garlic, finely
  crushed
225g (8oz) softened butter
2 heaped tablespoons
  chopped parsley
coarse sea salt and
  pepper

- Lay each lobster on a chopping board and cut in half lengthways. Crack the claws with the back of a heavy knife. These can be left attached or the meat removed and arranged in the head cavity of each half.

- Mix the garlic with the butter, parsley, salt and a twist of pepper in a food processor.

- Preheat the grill. Spread the lobsters liberally with the flavoured butter and arrange, shell-side down, on a baking tray. Place under the grill, not too close to the top, and grill for 6–7 minutes. Spoon the remaining garlic butter over each, providing plenty in the head shell ready for dipping.

lobster and orange salad in a green peppercorn dressing

serves **four**

2 x 750g (1lb 10oz)
  cooked lobsters
2 large oranges
150ml (5fl oz)
  natural yoghurt
1 tablespoon green
  peppercorns, in brine
½ teaspoon English or
  Dijon mustard
2 tablespoons olive oil
a splash of brandy
salt
100g (4oz) mixed
  salad leaves

The salad leaves are your choice, with chicory, curly endive, watercress, Little Gems, rocket or English butterheads just a few to choose from. For a simpler version, serve this salad with warm or cold prawns.

- Shell the lobsters and cut the meat into cubes. The claws can be cracked with the back of a heavy knife and the meat removed or left whole to garnish the salad.

- To segment the oranges, top and tail the fruits using a serrated edged knife. The rind and pith can now be removed by cutting in a sawing motion down the sides. To release the segments, simply cut between each membrane into segments, saving all the juices.

- To make the dressing, place the yoghurt, peppercorns, mustard, oil, brandy, orange juice and a pinch of salt in a food processor or blender and process until fairly smooth. Extra brandy, mustard or green peppercorns can be added for a stronger flavour. Pour into a screw-top jar and shake well before use. The dressing will keep refrigerated for up to 48 hours.

- Divide the lobster, orange segments and salad leaves among four plates and drizzle the green peppercorn dressing over each, garnishing with the lobster claws if using.

moules marinières

serves **four**

2kg (4½lb) mussels
75g (3oz) unsalted butter
1 large onion, finely
  chopped
1 glass of white wine
1 heaped tablespoon
  chopped parsley
a squeeze of lemon

- Clean the mussels by washing them under cold running water, scraping away any barnacles and pulling out the beards that protrude from between the closed shells. If any mussels are found slightly open, a short, sharp tap should make them close, letting you know they are still alive. Any that don't close should be discarded.

- Put the mussels, 25g (1oz) of the butter, the onion and white wine into a large saucepan (it's important that the saucepan is only half full of mussels for even cooking).

- Cover with a lid and cook over a high heat for 3–7 minutes, shaking the pan and stirring the mussels from time to time until they have all opened.

- Spoon the mussels into bowls, discarding any that have not opened. To finish, whisk the remaining butter, parsley and a squeeze of lemon into the cooking juices and spoon them over the steaming mussels.

and more

A few tablespoons of double cream can also be whisked into the juices to create a more silky smooth result.

scallops with asparagus and parma ham crackling

serves **four** as a starter

16–20 asparagus spears
salt and pepper
olive oil, for cooking
4 slices of Parma ham
12 scallops, out of shell
6 tablespoons sour cream
  or crème fraîche
a knob of butter

• Snap the woody end from each asparagus spear and discard, drop into a large pan of boiling salted water and cook for several minutes until tender. Drain and season with salt and pepper.

• Meanwhile, warm the olive oil in a large frying pan over a medium heat. Put the Parma ham slices in the pan and fry for a few minutes on both sides until they have become crisp like crackling. Remove the rashers, keeping them warm to one side.

• Season the scallops with salt and pepper, place them in the hot pan and fry over a high heat for 1–1½ minutes until golden brown. Turn and repeat the same cooking time on the other side.

• Spoon the sour cream on to the plates, then brush the asparagus spears with the butter before laying them on top. Arrange the scallops on the asparagus, topping with the Parma ham crackling.

and more

Lime or lemon juice can be added to the sour cream for a sharper citrus flavour.

A few teaspoons of tarragon vinegar can be whisked into a few tablespoons of olive oil for an instant dressing to spoon over.

calamari with hot ratatouille

serves **four**

450g (1lb) cleaned
 baby squid
2 tomatoes
90ml (3½fl oz) olive oil
1 tablespoon
 red wine vinegar
coarse sea salt
 and pepper
1 tablespoon finely
 chopped chives
1 green pepper,
 thinly sliced
1 red pepper, thinly sliced
1 large clove of
 garlic, crushed
1 small or ½ a medium
 aubergine, cut into
 small pieces
2 small–medium
 courgettes, thinly sliced

- Cut the squid into rings and cut the tentacles into smaller pieces if they are large in size.

- With the point of a knife, remove the eye from the tomatoes. Place in a bowl, cover with boiling water and leave to stand for just 10–15 seconds before placing under cold running water. Peel away the skin, quarter the tomatoes, deseed and cut the flesh into cubes.

- To make the dressing, whisk together 3 tablespoons of the olive oil and the red wine vinegar, seasoning with salt and pepper before stirring in the tomatoes and chives.

- Heat 2 tablespoons of the olive oil in a wok or large frying pan. Once hot, add the peppers, garlic, aubergine and courgettes. Fry for a couple of minutes until the vegetables are just beginning to soften.

- Push the vegetables to one side of the wok or frying pan and add the remaining olive oil to the empty side. Add the squid rings and tentacles and fry for 30 seconds before mixing with the ratatouille. Cook together for a further minute, season with salt and pepper and spoon over the dressing.

and more

Served over baby spinach leaves, this dish becomes a salad for a starter or light supper.

The simple wok-fried ratatouille can be made without the squid and stirred into noodles, couscous or rice for a filling meal.

squid tempura with a mango chutney dip

serves **four**

16–18 cleaned baby squid
150ml (5fl oz)
  natural yoghurt
a squeeze of lime
3–4 tablespoons
  mango chutney
90g (3½oz) plain flour,
  plus extra for dusting
15g (½oz) cornflour
¼ teaspoon
  bicarbonate of soda
salt
oil, for deep-frying

- Cut the squid into rings or halve them lengthways, cutting each half into strips.

- To make the dip, mix together the yoghurt, lime juice and chutney. If you want a smoother dip, blitz the lot in a food processor or blender.

- Measure 200ml (7fl oz) water into a bowl and add a large handful of ice. Leave to stand for a few minutes before remeasuring 200ml (7fl oz) ice-cold water.

- Put the flour, cornflour, bicarbonate of soda and a pinch of salt into a bowl and stir in the water to give you a loose batter.

- Heat at least 6cm (2½ inches) oil in a large pan, wok or deep-fat fryer to 180°C (350°F). Lightly dust the squid strips with flour, tapping away any excess, then briefly dip each into the batter, coating very lightly. Drop the squid into the hot oil, a few at a time, and fry for just 1–2 minutes until crisp and a pale golden brown. Drain on kitchen paper.

- The crispy tempura can be offered on separate plates or served in one large pile with a bowl of the dip to accompany.

and more

You can also make a spicy squid tempura by replacing a teaspoon of the flour with a teaspoon of medium curry powder for that modern British classic: curry and mango chutney.

fish seafood poultry **pork**
lamb beef vegetables
pasta and rice eggs and
cheese desserts

creamy white wine sauce

makes **200ml** (7fl oz)

150ml (5fl oz) white wine
150ml (5fl oz)
  chicken stock
1 heaped
  teaspoon cornflour
100ml (3½fl oz)
  whipping cream
a squeeze of lemon
salt and pepper

This sauce is ideal for poached or steamed chicken and pork and can also be applied to fish by exchanging the chicken stock for fish stock.

- Boil the white wine and stock together until just two-thirds of the liquid is left.

- Loosen the cornflour with a little cold water and whisk it into the sauce, simmering for a few minutes.

- Stir in the cream and simmer the sauce for a few more minutes, then add the lemon juice and season with salt and pepper.

mushroom sauce

makes **400ml** (14fl oz)

a knob of butter
½ onion, very
  finely chopped
175g (6oz) button
  mushrooms, sliced
1 glass of white wine
150ml (5fl oz) double
  or whipping cream
salt and pepper

This sauce enhances a simple chicken breast, pork chop or piece of poached fish.

- Melt the butter in a saucepan. Once bubbling, add the onion and mushrooms and cook for several minutes over a low heat until tender.

- Add the white wine, bring to the boil and boil until just half the liquid is left.

- Add the cream and cook for a few minutes. Season with salt and pepper.

and more

A squeeze of lemon can be added to the mushrooms to maintain their whiteness.

A tablespoon of Madeira wine can be added to the finished sauce for a richer taste.

roast chicken with gravy

serves **four**

1.6–1.8kg (3½–4lb)
  chicken
50g (2oz) softened butter
salt and pepper
300ml (10fl oz) chicken
  stock or consommé

• Preheat the oven to 200°C/400°F/gas 6. Brush the chicken all over with the butter and season with salt and pepper.

• Place the chicken in a roasting tray, breast-side down, and roast for 40 minutes, basting from time to time. Turn the bird breast-side up, baste liberally and roast for a further 20 minutes. To see if the bird is cooked, pierce between the thigh and breast with a skewer and check that the juices run clear. Transfer the bird on to a plate, breast-side down, and leave to rest for 15 minutes.

• Return the roasting tray to the stove. Once sizzling, pour in the stock, stirring to loosen the sticky juices from the base of the tray. Simmer for a few minutes, seasoning with salt and pepper before straining through a sieve. Carve the chicken into thick pieces to retain maximum moistness and serve with the gravy.

and more

The gravy can be thickened by whisking in 1–2 teaspoons cornflour, loosened with a little water, and simmering for a few minutes before serving.

roast chicken trimmings

bacon and chipolatas

serves **four**

4–8 rashers of streaky
  bacon or pancetta
8–12 chipolatas

- The bacon can be fried or grilled until crispy and served alongside the chicken. Alternatively, lay the bacon over the chicken's breast while roasting to help maintain succulence, the bacon fat adding to the flavour of the juices. If trying this method, the bird should be roasted breast-side up for the entire time.

- The chipolatas can be added to the roasting tray during the last 20 minutes of cooking.

sage, onion and lemon stuffing

serves **four**

1 large onion,
  finely chopped
100g (4oz)
  sausages, skinned
finely grated zest and juice
  of 1 lemon
1 tablespoon
  chopped sage
100g (4oz) fresh
  white breadcrumbs
1 beaten egg
salt and pepper

- Mix together the onion, sausage meat, lemon zest and juice, sage, breadcrumbs, egg and some salt and pepper in a bowl or food processor.

- Preheat the oven to 200°C/400°F/gas 6. Put the stuffing into a buttered dish and roast for 30–40 minutes. The stuffing can also be placed in the cavity formed by gently releasing the skin at the neck end of the chicken. Replace the skin over the stuffing and secure with a small skewer or cocktail stick before roasting.

bread sauce

serves **four**

1 small onion, peeled and
  halved
4 cloves
1 bay leaf
300ml (10fl oz) milk
50g (2oz) fresh white
  breadcrumbs
a knob of butter
2 tablespoons double
  cream
salt and pepper
a pinch of grated nutmeg

- Stud the onion halves with the cloves. Place the studded onions and bay leaf in the milk and bring to a simmer. Remove the pan from the heat, cover with a lid and leave to infuse for 1 hour.

- When ready to serve, remove the onions and bay leaf. Stir in the breadcrumbs and warm over a low heat for 5–10 minutes until the crumbs are swollen and the sauce thickens.

- Add the butter and cream and season with the salt, pepper and nutmeg.

roast chicken wing kiev

serves **four** as a snack

1kg (2¼lb) chicken wings
salt and pepper
4–5 tablespoons olive oil
75g (3oz) fresh
  white breadcrumbs
100g (4oz) garlic and
  parsley butter
  (see page 215)
150ml (5fl oz) sour cream
  or crème fraîche
  (optional)

This is the same combination of flavours as a chicken Kiev, but the recipe takes on a different identity with the garlic and herb butter spooned over the wings. Make into a complete meal with a salad.

• Preheat the oven to 200°C/400°F/gas 6. In a large roasting tray, season the wings with salt and pepper and mix in 2–3 tablespoons of the olive oil. Roast in the oven, turning from time to time, for 30–35 minutes until cooked through and well coloured. The chicken wings can be cooked for up to 1 hour for extra crispy skin.

• While roasting the wings, fry the breadcrumbs in a frying pan with the remaining olive oil until golden and crispy.

• Cut the garlic and parsley butter into pieces and spoon over the chicken wings with the crispy breadcrumbs. Serve with the sour cream to dip into, if using.

chicken with wholegrain mustard asparagus

serves **four**

12 chicken thighs, skin on
salt and pepper
75g (3oz) butter
12–16 asparagus spears
1 tablespoon
 wholegrain mustard
juice of ½ lemon

• Preheat the oven to 200°C/400°F/gas 6. Season the chicken thighs with salt and pepper. Heat an ovenproof frying pan or roasting tray on top of the stove with 25g (1oz) of the butter. Once it begins to sizzle, lay in the chicken, skin-side down, and fry over a medium heat for a few minutes to a golden brown. Turn the thighs and bake in the oven for 20 minutes, basting from time to time.

• Snap the woody end from each asparagus spear, cut the spears in three, drop into a large pan of boiling salted water and cook for several minutes until tender. Spoon the cooked spears into a shallow pan along with 4–5 tablespoons of the cooking water and bring to a simmer. Add the mustard and remaining butter, stirring it well, and return to a gentle simmer.

• Remove the cooked chicken from the oven and turn the pieces in the lemon juice. Arrange in a large serving dish, pouring any lemony juices into the mustard butter asparagus and scooping the lot over and around the chicken.

crispy parmesan chicken with soft basil tomatoes

serves **four**

4 chicken breasts,
 skinless
salt and pepper
flour, for dusting
75g (3oz) fresh
 white breadcrumbs
50g (2oz) finely grated
 Parmesan cheese
2 beaten eggs
olive oil, for cooking
a large knob of butter
6 tomatoes, halved
1–2 cloves of garlic,
 thinly sliced
coarse sea salt
a handful of basil leaves
4 wedges of lemon

- Lightly bat the chicken breasts between sheets of clingfilm until about 5mm–1cm (¼–½ inch) thick. Season with salt and pepper, then dust in flour to coat, tapping away any excess. Mix together the breadcrumbs and Parmesan. Dip the escalopes in the beaten egg, followed by the Parmesan breadcrumbs.

- Heat some olive oil with the butter in a large frying pan. Once sizzling, add the crumbed escalopes and cook for 3–4 minutes on each side until crispy and golden.

- Preheat the grill and put the tomato halves on a baking tray, topping each with a slice of garlic. Season with a good twist of pepper and a sprinkling of sea salt. Drizzle with olive oil and grill until just overdone, their softness providing the escalopes with a sauce to dip into.

- Tear the basil leaves and scatter them over the tomatoes with a drizzle of olive oil. Serve with the escalopes and a wedge of lemon.

sticky lemon chicken pieces

serves **four**

4 large chicken legs
salt and pepper
olive oil, for cooking
1 tablespoon light soft
  brown sugar
finely grated zest and juice
  of 1 large lemon
50g (2oz) butter,
  cut into cubes

The cooking time in this recipe may seem a bit long for chicken pieces, but this is intentional, the succulent meat just falling off the bone.

• Preheat the oven to 200°C/400°F/gas 6. Season the chicken legs with salt and pepper. Heat an ovenproof braising pan or roasting tray on top of the stove with some olive oil and lay in the chicken, skin-side down. Fry for a few minutes until golden brown before turning each piece.

• Mix together the sugar and lemon zest, sprinkle it over the chicken and place the pan in the oven. Roast, basting from time to time, for 35–40 minutes.

• Remove the pan from the oven, squeeze over the lemon juice and drop in the butter. Arrange the chicken pieces on plates and spoon the lemony butter all over.

and more

Chicken thighs, drumsticks or halved chicken legs all suit this dish.

This tasty chicken dish works very well with a simple green salad.

chicken with porcini and chestnut mushrooms

serves **four**

25g (1oz) sliced dried
  porcini mushrooms
4 chicken breasts, skin on
salt and pepper
olive oil, for cooking
a knob of butter
1 heaped tablespoon
  finely chopped shallots
  or onion
100g (4oz) chestnut
  mushrooms, sliced
100–150ml (3½–5fl oz)
  double cream
juice of ½ lemon
1 tablespoon chopped
  flat-leaf parsley

Porcini is the Italian word for cep mushrooms, available fresh during our autumn months. They can also be found dried, as I'm using here, throughout the year. Chestnut mushrooms have become quite common on our shelves, their flavour adding a nutty edge.

- Soak the porcini mushrooms for 20–30 minutes in 300ml (10fl oz) warm water. Once softened, scoop the mushrooms from the water, squeezing any excess juices back into the bowl, and keep the mushroom-flavoured water to one side.

- Season the chicken breasts with salt and pepper and place them, skin-side down, in a preheated frying pan with some olive oil and the knob of butter. Fry over a medium heat for 5–7 minutes on each side until cooked and golden brown. Lift from the pan and keep warm to one side.

- Add the shallots, porcini and chestnut mushrooms to the pan, frying for a couple of minutes. Pour in the saved mushroom water, except the last couple of tablespoons, which tend to have impurities. Boil until just half the liquid is left, then add the cream and return to a simmer, cooking the sauce for a few more minutes until slightly thickened.

- Season the sauce and add the lemon juice and parsley. Pop the chicken breasts back into the pan along with any juices and serve.

roast paprika chicken

serves **four**

1.6–1.8kg (3½–4lb)
  chicken
50g (2oz) softened butter
salt
1 lemon, halved
1 tablespoon paprika

• Preheat the oven to 200°C/400°F/gas 6. Brush the chicken all over with the butter and season with salt. Squeeze over the lemon juice, then dust the chicken with paprika.

• Place the chicken in a roasting tray, breast-side up, and roast for 1 hour, basting from time to time. To see if the bird is cooked, pierce between the thigh and breast with a skewer and check that the juices run clear. Transfer the bird on to a plate breast-side down, pour over the juices from the tray and leave to rest for 15 minutes.

• Carve the chicken into thick pieces to retain maximum moistness, then spoon the juices over the meat.

and more

Adding 1–2 spoonfuls of sour cream to the juices blends very well with the paprika.

For garlic, herb and lemon chicken, leave out the paprika, and add 2 tablespoons chopped mixed herbs (parsley, thyme, tarragon, chives), 1 large clove of crushed garlic and the zest of 1 lemon to 75g (3oz) butter before rubbing all over the chicken.

chicken livers with a sweet spinach and bacon salad

serves **four** as a starter

1 heaped tablespoon
 mincemeat
4 tablespoons walnut oil
8–12 chicken livers
4 rashers of streaky bacon
coarse sea salt
 and pepper
olive oil, for cooking
1–2 handfuls of baby
 spinach

The mincemeat is the kind we use for Christmas mince pies. Once puréed with the walnut oil, the spicy fruit flavour contrasts well with the peppery livers.

- Put the mincemeat, walnut oil and 4 tablespoons water into a food processor or blender and blitz to a smooth sauce consistency, with dots of black raisin still visible. Trim the chicken livers and place them on kitchen paper to dry.

- Preheat the grill. Lay the bacon rashers on a grill tray with a rack and place under the grill, not too close to the top, and cook until golden and crispy.

- Season the livers with a good twist of pepper. Heat some olive oil in a non-stick frying pan and fry the livers for just a few minutes until golden brown on both sides. Season with a sprinkling of sea salt, remove from the pan and leave to rest.

- Spoon some of the dressing on to the plates and scatter over the spinach leaves and chicken livers. Drizzle a little more dressing over and top with a rasher of warm crispy bacon.

roasted turkey with a warm mushroom salad

serves **four**

1kg (2¼lb) boneless
  turkey breast, skin
  removed
salt and pepper
olive oil, for cooking
50g (2oz) butter
6 little gem lettuces,
  halved
100g (4oz) button
  mushrooms, sliced
1 tablespoon
  white wine vinegar
150ml (5fl oz)
  crème fraîche
1 tablespoon
  chopped chives

It's not essential to roast your own turkey; lovely carved-by-hand fresh turkey is available in most supermarkets. Roast chicken or slices of ham work equally well.

• Preheat the oven to 200°C/400°F/gas 6. Season the turkey with salt and pepper. Heat a roasting tray with some oil and fry the turkey on all sides to a light golden brown. Remove from the heat and transfer the turkey into the centre of a large sheet of foil, spooning over any oil left in the pan and topping with the butter. Seal the foil before returning the turkey to the tray and baking for 55–60 minutes.

• Once cooked, remove the turkey from the tray and leave to rest for 20–30 minutes until just warm.

• Bring a large saucepan of water to the boil, adding 2 teaspoons salt. Plunge the Little Gems into the boiling water and cook for 30–60 seconds until only just beginning to soften. Spoon the lettuces into a colander and leave to drain.

• Put the mushrooms into a frying pan with the vinegar and simmer until softened. Stir in the crème fraîche and chives and, once warm, add the lettuce halves, turning them to coat with the mushroom dressing. Season with salt and pepper.

• Open the foil bag and remove the turkey, saving any buttery juices. Carve the breast into two to three slices per portion and drizzle with the juices. Divide the salad among the plates, spoon over the cream dressing and top with the turkey slices.

and more

A teaspoon of English or Dijon mustard can be added to the crème fraîche.

treacle duck breasts with creamy date parsnips

serves **four**

900g (2lb) parsnips,
  peeled and quartered
100g (4oz) dates, halved
  and stoned
milk
salt and ground white
  pepper
4 duck breasts
1 tablespoon oil
150ml (5fl oz) madeira or
  red wine
400ml (14fl oz) tin of game
  or beef consommé or
  chicken stock
1–2 teaspoons cornflour
1 tablespoon black treacle

Although not essential, the wrinkled, toffee-like medjool dates are the best to use for this dish. I've also included a rich sauce, which isn't strictly needed as the date parsnips are very moist, but does add a tasty extra if you want to make it.

• Cut away the woody core from each of the parsnip quarters and place the parsnips in a saucepan with the dates, pouring over enough milk to cover. Bring to a simmer and cook for 15–20 minutes until the parsnips are completely tender. To make the parsnip purée, spoon the parsnips and dates into a blender and blitz until smooth, adding some of the milk if needed to loosen. Season with the salt and pepper.

• Preheat the oven to 220°C/425°F/gas 7. Season the duck breasts with salt and pepper and heat the oil in a roasting tray on top of the stove. Place the breasts, skin-side down, in the tray and fry over a medium heat for 8–10 minutes, allowing the skin to release fat while turning golden brown. Turn and finish cooking in the oven for 7–8 minutes. Remove from the tray and leave to rest.

• Meanwhile, boil the Madeira in a small saucepan until just a third of the liquid is left. Pour in the consommé and simmer for a few minutes. Loosen the cornflour with a little water and whisk in, a little at a time, until a sauce consistency is reached.

• Preheat the grill. Loosen the treacle with a little water, arrange the duck breasts on a baking tray and brush lightly with the treacle. Grill until the treacle begins to sizzle, brushing each breast once more, then serve whole or cut into three to four slices with the hot creamy date parsnips and the sauce.

roasted duck with red wine blackberries

serves **four**

2 x 1.5kg (3lb 5oz) ducks
salt and pepper
2 glasses of fruity red wine
2 teaspoons soft brown or
   demerara sugar
5 tablespoons blackberry
   jam or jelly
175g (6oz) blackberries
50g (2oz) butter

In this recipe, the legs and breasts are carved off the duck to serve, but if you have poultry shears, they can be used to divide the ducks in two, serving each person half a duck.

• Preheat the oven to 220°C/425°F/gas 7. Place the ducks in a large roasting tray and sprinkle each with salt before roasting for 20 minutes in the oven.

• Reduce the oven temperature to 180°C/350°F/gas 4. Baste the birds and continue to roast for a further 1 hour 40 minutes, basting from time to time.

• Remove the ducks from the tray and leave to rest for 10–15 minutes. To serve, cut the legs and the breasts from each duck, offering one of each per person.

• While the ducks are resting, boil the wine with the sugar in a saucepan until just two-thirds of the liquid is left. Stir in the jam and gently warm through until the jam is completely melted.

• Add the blackberries and butter to the sauce and simmer for a few minutes until the fruits have softened. Season with salt and pepper. Spoon the sauce over the duck to serve.

and more

Mashed or sauté potatoes work well with this dish.

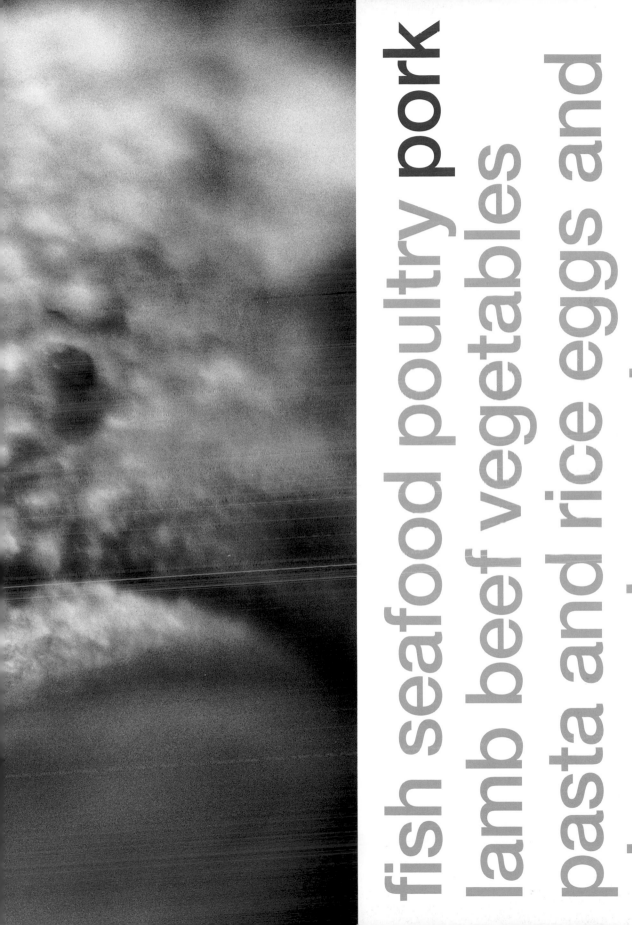

fish seafood poultry **pork** lamb beef vegetables pasta and rice eggs and cheese desserts

keeping pork simple

The amazing thing about a pig is that you can eat almost every bit of it and that means there's a huge repertoire of dishes to choose from. It's an incredible beast and a superb white meat. It also takes on all of the flavours chicken can, so if you want to swap pork for the chicken in any of the recipes, just pick a cut from the list below.

how to choose pork

When you're buying pork, make sure the meat is moist but never over oily.

A high fat content is essential to the most beautiful cuts of pork. Don't be afraid of it because it helps tenderize the meat.

If you can get hold of a specially reared breed, like Gloucester Old Spot, it will be fabulous to eat because its free lifestyle produces a richer flavour.

British pork in general is very good, but you will get better quality if you pick outdoor-reared pork.

pork cuts

Without question, belly is my favourite cut of pork because the tenderizing layers of fat guarantee moistness. The only way to cook it is by slow roasting until it almost melts.

The loin is almost like chicken breast and can be dry, so be careful not to overcook it.

The leg is best slow-roasted. It can be divided into joints, but the prime cut is the lean fillet, which can be bought ready for roasting.

The problem with pork chops is that by the time the skin gets crispy, the meat can be overcooked. To start the cooking evenly, stand them up in the pan with the fat on the base.

Fillet is excellent for stir-fries. You can use almost any lean cut for the many quick-fried pork dishes, but do make sure you always cook the meat fast and hot enough.

Shoulder is a great cut for pot-roasting. Buy it boned, rolled and tied and it will baste itself.

A gammon steak with 2 fried eggs is a breakfast favourite. I prefer unsmoked gammon and I like to pan-fry or grill it and serve with a slice of fresh peppered pineapple.

I prefer unsmoked bacon to smoked, but I also often substitute cubes of smoky Italian pancetta for bacon when I'm cooking.

Sausages. Wonderful British food, Lincolnshire sausages are my favourite at the moment.

a charcuterie lunch

Charcuterie, meaning any of Europe's delicious ready-prepared cured meats, pâtés or terrines, particularly those made from pork, can make an easy little starter or be put together to create a fabulous instant meal. For a lesson in delicious simplicity, go to your supermarket or local deli and create a whole meal from all the charcuterie choices now available. Below are some of the things that would be in my basket:

A good thick slice of smoked York ham or any other British ham

A pot of English mustard

Crusty bread for slicing

Thin slices of Italian and Hungarian salami

A few pickles

Chicken liver pâté

Paper-thin slices of raw Italian Parma ham

Air-dried Spanish jamon serrano, mountain ham, preferably hand-carved, or the wonderful, but often very expensive, jamon Iberico

Good old-fashioned corned or salt beef or pastrami

Sliced bresaola, cured Italian beef, with a drizzle of olive oil and a squeeze of lemon

simple sauces for pork

apple sauce

serves **four–six**

3 Bramley apples,
  peeled, cored and
  roughly chopped
1 tablespoon lemon juice
25g (1oz) butter
1 tablespoon caster sugar
  (optional)

This apple sauce can be left quite natural and chunky or blended until smooth and sweetened with caster sugar if preferred. Serve with roast pork.

• Place the apples in a saucepan with 2 tablespoons water and the lemon juice and cook over a low heat for 10–15 minutes until softened.

• Stir in the butter and sugar, if using.

• The sauce can be left chunky or put into a blender and whisked to a smooth consistency.

mustard sauce

makes **200ml** (7fl oz)

300ml (10fl oz) chicken
  stock
150ml (5fl oz) double
  cream
2–3 teaspoons English,
  Dijon or wholegrain
  mustard
salt and pepper
a squeeze of lemon

This is a simple, tasty replacement for gravy to serve
with pork or poultry.

• Place the stock in a saucepan, bring to the boil and boil until just
  half the liquid is left to intensify the flavour.

• Add the double cream and simmer until the sauce thickens.

• Whisk in the mustard and season with salt and pepper. Squeeze
  in a little lemon juice to sharpen the sauce.

and more

A knob of butter can be whisked into the sauce for a richer flavour
or alternatively a tablespoon of chopped herbs, such as parsley
or chives, can be added.

pork chops with an apple tart topping

serves **four**

7–8 Cox's apples
25g (1oz) caster sugar
juice of ½ lemon
4 pork chops
25g (1oz) butter,
  half melted
salt and pepper

There is no pastry included here; the topping is made up purely of a chunky apple sauce and sliced apples arranged like an apple tart. The apple sauce recipe is given below, but using a quality bought product would make this recipe one of the easiest in the book.

- Peel, core and roughly chop four of the apples and put into a saucepan. Add half the caster sugar, the lemon juice and 3 tablespoons water, cover with a lid and cook over a medium to low heat for 10–15 minutes until tender, stirring from time to time. The topping can be left very chunky or lightly whisked until smoother. Cover and keep warm.

- Preheat the grill. Brush the pork chops with a little of the firm half of the butter and season with salt and pepper. Put the chops onto a grill tray with a rack, place under the grill and cook for 4–5 minutes on each side.

- While grilling the chops, peel, quarter and core the remaining apples. Cut into long thin slices, maintaining the shape of the apple. Spread the apple sauce over the chops and arrange the apple slices on top, slightly overlapping as you would for an apple tart. Brush or drizzle the chops with the melted butter, sprinkle over the remaining sugar and return to the grill. Cook for a few minutes until the apples are nicely toasted with a slightly burnt tinge around the edges.

and more

The lemon juice can be replaced with 1–2 tablespoons Calvados.

pork stroganoff

serves **four**

a knob of butter
1 onion, sliced
100g (4oz) button
  mushrooms, sliced
350g (12oz) pork fillet, cut
  into thin strips
salt
a pinch of cayenne pepper
a pinch of paprika
2–3 tablespoons brandy
1 teaspoon Dijon mustard
100–150ml (3½–5fl oz)
  sour cream or
  crème fraîche

The pork fillet is the same tender, lean joint as beef fillet.
If unavailable, thin strips of pork loin can also be used.

• Melt the knob of butter in a wok or large frying pan. Once
  sizzling, add the onion and mushroom and fry for a few minutes
  until softened.

• Season the pork fillet strips with salt, cayenne pepper and
  paprika. Scatter the strips into the pan, increasing the heat and
  cooking for several minutes with the onion and mushroom.

• Pour in and flambé the brandy in the pan. Stir in the Dijon
  mustard before pouring in the sour cream. Simmer for a minute,
  seasoning with more salt, cayenne pepper and paprika, if needed.

and more

A red pepper cut into thin strips can be added and fried with the
onion and mushroom until tender.

Serve with braised rice (see page 309) or mash (see page 250).

pork belly boulangère

serves **four**

1kg (2¼lb) pork belly
coarse sea salt and
  pepper
oil, for brushing
4 large baking potatoes,
  peeled and thinly sliced
2 large onions, sliced
600ml (1 pint) chicken
  stock

Pork belly can roast in just 1½ hours. However, for an almost buttery texture, it is best to double the cooking time as you'll find here. This might sound time-consuming, but the cooking couldn't be easier. For a crunchier crackling, ask your butcher to score the skin.

• Preheat the oven to 160°C/325°F/gas 3. Season the meat side of the pork belly with salt and pepper and place the joint, skin-side up, on a roasting tray with a rack. Brush the skin with oil, sprinkle liberally with coarse sea salt and roast in the oven for 3 hours.

• With the pork in the oven, mix the potatoes with the onions and spoon into a shallow baking dish or roasting tray large enough to sit beneath the pork and capture all of the released juices. Pour over the chicken stock.

• After the first hour of roasting the pork, exchange the roasting tray beneath the rack with the potato. Continue to roast for the final 2 hours. At the end of the cooking time, if the potatoes have only coloured slightly, they can be placed under a hot grill until they turn a rich golden brown.

• Cut the crackling from the belly, snapping it into large pieces. Carve the pork in thick slices, dividing it among the plates along with a generous spoonful of potatoes and chunk of crackling.

and more

A couple of large crushed or sliced garlic cloves can be added to the potato and onion mix.

white pork and wild mushroom stew

serves **four**

50g (2oz) dried
  wild mushrooms
900g (2lb) diced pork
a large knob of butter
2 onions, finely chopped
salt and pepper
1 glass of white wine
150ml (5fl oz)
  double cream
a squeeze of lemon
1 heaped tablespoon
  roughly chopped chervil

While fresh wild mushrooms are only available during the autumn and winter months, good-quality wild mushrooms are available year-round. Here I've chosen the wrinkly morels, although a big bag of mixed wild mushrooms would be equally great.

- Soak the dried mushrooms in 600ml (1 pint) warm water for 20 minutes. Remove the mushrooms, reserving the soaking water, and trim the stalks. Rinse lightly under cold water to remove any grit and keep to one side.

- Put the pork into a large saucepan and cover with water. Bring to a simmer and cook for 5 minutes. Drain the meat and rinse under cold running water.

- Return the pan to the stove and melt the butter. When sizzling, add the onion and cook over a medium heat until it begins to soften without colouring. Season the pork with salt and pepper, then return to the pan. Strain over the mushroom water, pour in the wine and bring to a simmer. Lower the heat, cover with a lid, and simmer for 1¾ hours until the meat is tender.

- Add the mushrooms, pour in the cream and return to a fairly rapid simmer until the sauce is slightly thicker. Check the seasoning and add the lemon juice to taste. Scatter with the chervil and serve.

and more

Half a chicken stock cube can be sprinkled into the cooking juices to enrich the flavour.

smoky bacon, potato and gruyère frittata

serves **four**

2 medium–large potatoes, quartered
225g (8oz) cubes of smoked bacon or pancetta
25g (1oz) butter
6 spring onions, finely chopped
6 eggs
100g (4oz) Gruyère cheese, grated
salt and pepper

A frittata is an Italian flat omelette, called a tortilla in Spain, which is completely cooked through unlike the soft-centred French omelette.

• Cook the potatoes in boiling salted water for approximately 20–25 minutes until cooked through. Drain and leave to cool slightly before peeling and cutting into cubes.

• Heat a non-stick frying pan, preferably 20cm (8 inches) in diameter. Fry the bacon until golden brown, then drain off any excess fat before adding the butter and potatoes with half the spring onions. Cook for a few minutes over a low heat.

• Beat the eggs, adding half the grated cheese. Season with the salt and pepper. Pour the eggs into the pan, stirring them into the bacon and potatoes. Stir gently in the pan for a few minutes, allowing the frittata to cook over a very low heat until it begins to set, leaving just a moist surface. Preheat the grill.

• Sprinkle the remaining spring onions and cheese on top and warm under the grill until the top has set and the cheese melted. Cut the frittata into wedges to serve.

grilled gammon with pear mayonnaise and a chicory salad

serves **four**

2 large ripe pears
a knob of butter
a squeeze of lime
3 tablespoons mayonnaise
2 small chicory heads
1 bag of watercress
12 walnut halves,
  quartered
1 teaspoon clear honey
1 tablespoon sherry
  vinegar
2 tablespoons walnut oil
2 tablespoons sunflower
  or groundnut oil
salt and pepper
4 x 175g (6oz) gammon
  steaks
olive oil, for brushing

The pear-flavoured mayonnaise is an alternative to the regular pairing of gammon and apple, but if you do fancy apple, simply take a small jar of smooth apple sauce and whisk with 1–2 tablespoons mayonnaise.

• Peel, quarter, core and roughly chop the pears, popping them into a saucepan with the butter and lime juice. Cook over a low heat for a few minutes until tender and beginning to purée naturally, then whisk in a blender until smooth. Leave to cool. Once cold, whisk in the mayonnaise.

• Separate the chicory leaves and mix together with the watercress and walnuts in a bowl. To make the dressing, whisk the honey, sherry vinegar and the two oils, seasoning with salt and pepper.

• Preheat a ridged griddle pan or grill. Using scissors or a sharp knife, snip a few times around the gammon rinds to prevent the steaks from curling as they cook. Brush each with olive oil and season with a twist of pepper. Grill the steaks for 3–4 minutes on each side.

• Arrange the steaks on plates, drizzle the dressing over the salad leaves and offer the salad and pear mayonnaise for everyone to help themselves.

and more

A couple of tablespoons of crème fraîche or sour cream can be added to the salad dressing.

fish seafood poultry pork **lamb** beef vegetables pasta and rice eggs and cheese desserts

lamb cutlets with crispy sage and capers

serves **four**

oil, for cooking
1 bunch of sage leaves
salt and pepper
12 lamb cutlets
25–50g (1–2oz) softened
  butter
75ml (3fl oz) olive oil
1 tablespoon lemon juice
2 tablespoons capers

Lamb cutlets can be a little fatty and it is best to trim a bit of the excess fat if you find this to be the case.

- Heat a frying pan with 1cm (½ inch) oil and, once hot, fry the sage leaves, dropping in a small handful at a time. When the leaves are cooked and crispy, they will almost stop sizzling and become virtually stagnant in the pan. Lift out and drain on kitchen paper, seasoning with a pinch of salt.

- Preheat the grill. Place the lamb cutlets on a grill tray with a rack, brush with half the butter and season with salt and pepper. Cook under the grill for 3–5 minutes on each side, depending on how pink you prefer them, brushing with the remaining butter once turned.

- While grilling the cutlets, whisk together the olive oil, lemon juice and capers with a good twist of pepper. Arrange the cutlets on plates and pour any butter and juices from the grill tray into the caper dressing. Spoon the dressing over the lamb and sprinkle the crispy sage leaves on top.

and more

A few tablespoons of chopped tomatoes can be added to the caper dressing for a sweeter touch.

A nutty combination of 50ml (2fl oz) groundnut and 25ml (1fl oz) walnut or hazelnut oil can replace the olive oil.

The lamb cutlets are wonderful with sweet fresh or frozen peas.

roast leg of lamb

serves **four**

1.75kg (4lb) leg of lamb
olive oil, for cooking
salt and pepper
300ml (10fl oz) lamb,
  chicken or beef stock
1 tablespoon
  redcurrant jelly

Roast leg of lamb is a simple and versatile dish that can take on many flavours without masking or spoiling the sweet meat.

- Preheat the oven to 200°C/400°F/gas 6. Brush the leg with olive oil and season with salt and pepper.

- Place the leg in a roasting tray and cook and baste for 1 hour 15 minutes for medium rare, 1 hour 30 minutes for medium, 1 hour 45 minutes for medium well and 2 hours for well done. Remove the leg from the tray and leave to rest for 15–20 minutes.

- Pour off the fat from the roasting tray and heat the remaining juices until sizzling. Add the stock and bring to a simmer. Whisk in the redcurrant jelly until melted, then season with salt and pepper.

- Carve the lamb, offering the gravy as it is or straining it before serving.

and more

To make rosemary and garlic roast lamb, use a small knife to cut some deep incisions in the flesh side of the leg and insert a sprig of rosemary and a thick slice of garlic in each.

For a thicker gravy, whisk in 1–2 teaspoons of cornflour loosened with a little water.

lamb hotpot

serves **four**

oil, for cooking
8 large lamb chops
salt and pepper
25g (1oz) melted butter
4 potatoes, peeled
  and sliced
3 onions, sliced
4 carrots, sliced
1 large sprig of rosemary,
  finely chopped
600ml (1 pint)
  chicken stock

This is a complete meal baked under the same roof:
lamb chops, potatoes, carrots and onions. The classic
Lancashire hotpot also includes lambs' kidneys, which
have been left out here to keep the dish easy.

• Preheat the oven to 180°C/350°F/gas 4. Heat a frying pan with the
  oil, season the chops with salt and pepper and fry until well coloured.

• Brush a deep casserole dish with some of the butter. Scatter half
  of the potatoes across the base, followed by half the onions and
  carrots, then the fried chops, sprinkling them with the rosemary.
  Cover with the remaining carrots and onions, arranging the
  potatoes on top.

• Pour over the stock, cover with a lid and bake in the oven for
  2 hours. Remove the lid and brush the potatoes with the remaining
  melted butter. Increase the oven temperature to 200°C/400°F/gas
  6 and bake for a further 15–20 minutes to give a golden-brown
  edge to the potatoes.

slow-cooked red wine lamb shanks

serves **four**

4 small lamb shanks
salt and pepper
oil, for cooking
1 onion, sliced
1 large carrot,
  roughly chopped
2 cloves of garlic,
  chopped
2 bay leaves
1 sprig of rosemary
1 bottle of full-bodied
  red wine
400ml (14fl oz) tin of beef
  consommé or stock
1 tablespoon soft
  brown sugar
1–2 teaspoons cornflour
  (optional)

This lamb dish goes really well with the orange curd carrots (see page 282).

- Preheat the oven to 160°C/325°F/gas 3. Season the lamb shanks with salt and pepper. Heat a large braising pot with a little oil and fry the shanks until coloured all over, then remove from the pan and keep to one side.

- Put the onion, carrot, garlic, bay leaves and rosemary into the pan and cook gently until lightly coloured. Pour in the red wine and consommé, sprinkle in the sugar and bring to a simmer. Add the shanks, topping up with water if necessary, before returning to a simmer, covering with a lid and popping into the oven.

- Braise for 2½–3 hours until the meat almost wants to fall off the bone. At this point, remove the shanks from the pot and keep to one side. The cooking liquid can now be skimmed of any lamb fat. Should you prefer it thicker, the cornflour can be loosened with water and whisked in. The shanks and red wine sauce are now ready to serve.

apricot and pine nut rack of lamb with soft onions

serves **four**

2 racks of lamb
  (6–8 bones per rack),
  French trimmed
salt and pepper
1 heaped tablespoon
  pine nuts
4 thick slices of white
  bread, crusts removed
1 heaped teaspoon
  chopped lemon thyme
1 tablespoon
  chopped parsley
6 dried apricots,
  roughly chopped
40g (1½oz) melted butter
2 large onions, thinly sliced

This dish is perfect for an easy dinner party. There are few ingredients to work with and it looks very appealing. The fat covering a rack can be topped with the crust while still raw, however it is better to pan-fry it first to start the cooking and gain a better texture and flavour.

- Preheat the oven to 220°C/425°F/gas 7. Season the racks of lamb with salt and pepper. Heat a roasting tray on the stove and place the lamb in, fat-side down. Fry for a few minutes until well browned, then seal the racks on the meat side too before removing from the tray. Pour away most of the fat, leaving about a tablespoon in the pan.

- Preheat the grill. Toast the pine nuts under the grill until golden brown before roughly chopping. Mix crumbs made from the bread slices with the lemon thyme, parsley, apricots, pine nuts and melted butter, seasoning with salt and pepper. Pat the crumbs firmly on to each rack on the fat side, then return to the roasting tray, crumb-side up.

- For a pink finish, roast the racks for 15–20 minutes. Remove from the tray and keep the racks warm while they rest.

- Return the roasting tray to the stove, add the onion and fry for 5–10 minutes until the onions are coloured and soft and have absorbed any juices and roasted crumbs left in the tray. Season with salt and pepper.

- Cut the racks in half or divide into cutlets and serve them with the soft onions.

irish stew broth

serves **six**

450g (1lb) diced lean lamb
1 litre (1¾ pints)
  chicken stock
2 onions, sliced
1 bouquet garni
2 large potatoes, peeled
  and cut into chunks
2 carrots, peeled and sliced
¼ medium green cabbage
  or ½ a small one,
  finely shredded
salt and pepper
1 heaped tablespoon
  coarsely chopped parsley

- Put the lamb, chicken stock, onion and bouquet garni into a large saucepan. Bring to a simmer, cover partially with a lid and cook for 1¼ hours, skimming from time to time.

- Add the potatoes and carrots to the pot and continue to simmer for 20 minutes. Add the cabbage and simmer for 10 minutes. Remove the bouquet garni, season with salt and pepper and scatter over the parsley.

- The broth can now be ladled into bowls to serve.

west country squab pie

serves **four**

900g (2lb) lamb neck
  fillets, cut into 16 pieces
salt and pepper
1 onion, sliced
1 leek, sliced
8 prunes
2 Cox's apples, peeled,
  cored and sliced into
  wedges
2 thick slices of
  white bread
½ teaspoon
  ground allspice
a generous pinch
  of nutmeg
350g (12oz) ready rolled
  shortcrust or puff pastry
1 beaten egg

An easy-to-make pie from the West Country that doesn't actually contain any squab or wild pigeon, but was traditionally made with neck of mutton, here replaced with lamb neck fillets. Classically the pie is served with clotted cream.

• Preheat the oven to 200°C/400°F/gas 6. Season the lamb with salt and pepper before mixing in a 1.8 litre (3 pint) pie dish with the onion, leek, prunes and apples. Stir in breadcrumbs made from the slices of white bread and sprinkle over the allspice and nutmeg.

• Measure the pastry 4cm (1½ inches) larger than the pie dish. Moisten the rim of the dish with water and cut another strip of pastry to fit on to it. Brush the pastry-topped rim with the egg and lay the pastry over the dish, trimming off any excess. Press the edges together, brush the egg over the top and pierce a hole in the centre. Any pastry trimmings can be used to decorate the top.

• Leave to rest for 20 minutes, allowing the pastry to relax so it will not shrink while cooking. Bake for 20 minutes, then lower the oven temperature to 170°C/325°F/gas 3 and bake for a further 1¼ hours, the meat, vegetables and fruit creating their own gravy within the pie. Should the pastry begin to colour and brown too quickly, cover with a piece of foil to prevent it from burning.

liver steaks with crispy ham and marmalade onions

serves **four**

3 tablespoons olive oil
3 onions, sliced
2 teaspoons
  demerara sugar
300ml (10fl oz) red wine
1–2 tablespoons
  marmalade
salt and pepper
4 slices of cured ham
  (Parma, Bayonne or
  serrano)
4 x 175g (6oz) thick
  liver slices

We are used to quickly pan-frying thin liver, but here thicker liver slices are used for a more steak-like effect. However, the dish works equally well with thin liver slices. Lambs' or calves' livers can both be used.

- Heat a tablespoon of the olive oil in a large frying pan or wok. Once sizzling, add the onion and cook over a high heat until softened and well coloured. Stir in the demerara sugar and continue to fry for a couple of minutes, then pour over the red wine and boil until just half the liquid is left. Stir in the marmalade to thicken the sauce and season with a pinch of salt and a generous twist of pepper.

- Heat the remaining olive oil in a separate frying pan. Fry the cured ham over a medium heat for a few minutes until the slices become very crisp. Remove and drain on kitchen paper, keeping warm to one side.

- With the pan and oil still hot, add the liver steaks and fry for 2–3 minutes on each side, depending on their thickness, to leave them moist and pink inside. Season with salt and pepper and rest for a few minutes.

- Spoon the red wine onions on to plates with the steaks and ham.

and more

A green salad scattered with orange segments and drizzled with crème fraîche works very well with the liver, picking up the flavour of the marmalade.

cumberland kidneys on bitter rocket toasts

serves **four** as a starter

8 lambs' kidneys
1 teaspoon finely grated orange zest
1 teaspoon finely grated lemon zest
juice of 1 orange
juice of 1 lemon
1 tablespoon finely chopped shallots
4 tablespoons redcurrant jelly
4 tablespoons port
a pinch of ground ginger
salt and pepper
4 thick slices of crusty bread
a large knob of butter, plus extra for spreading
a handful of rocket leaves

The Cumberland in the title refers to the redcurrant, port and citrus-flavoured Cumberland sauce, a traditional partner for pâtés, terrines and game dishes.

- Cut each kidney into quarters and refrigerate until needed.

- Put the orange and lemon zest and juices into a saucepan with the shallots. Boil until just half the juice is left. Stir in the redcurrant jelly, port and ginger, simmering until the jelly has completely melted. Season with salt and pepper.

- Preheat the grill. Butter the bread slices on both sides. Toast under the grill until slightly burnt on both sides.

- Heat a frying pan with the knob of butter and once sizzling, add the kidneys, cooking over a high heat for 1–2 minutes for a medium-rare to medium result. Season with salt and pepper and transfer to a bowl.

- Stir in enough Cumberland sauce to coat the kidneys, offering any excess separately. Arrange the toasts on plates with the rocket leaves and top with the kidneys.

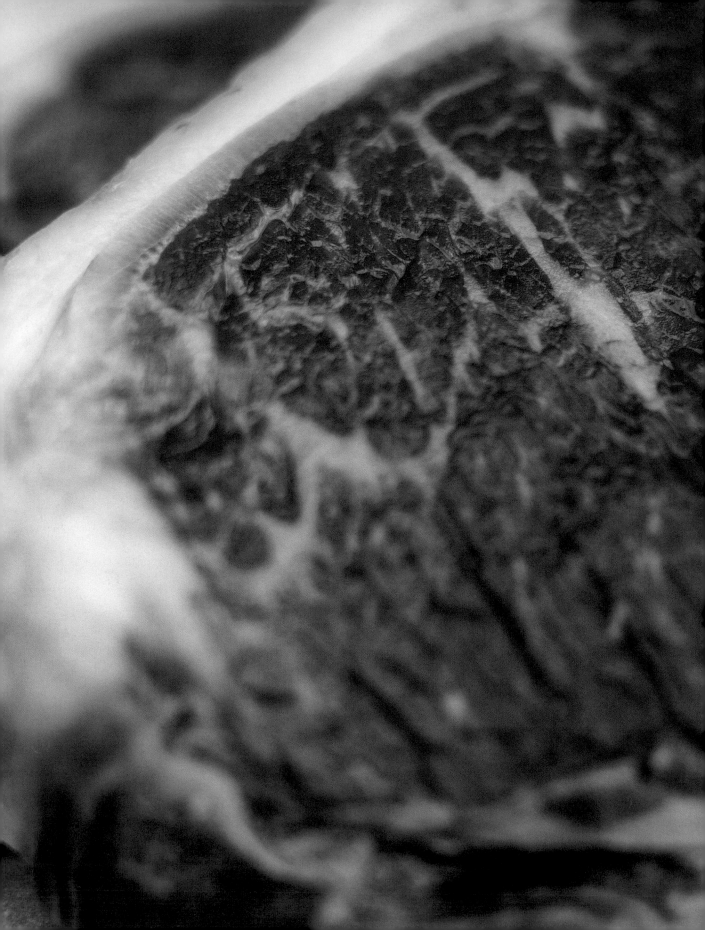

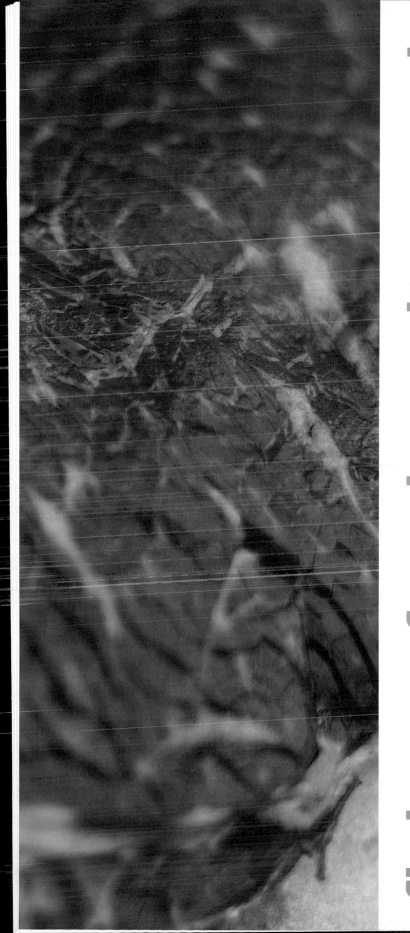

fish seafood poultry pork lamb **beef** vegetables pasta and rice eggs and cheese desserts

rump steak with home-made oven-baked garlic chips

serves **four**

900g (2lb) potatoes
4 tablespoons olive oil,
  plus extra for brushing
2 cloves of garlic,
  thinly sliced
salt and pepper
4 x 225g (8oz)
  rump steaks

- Preheat the oven to 200°C/400°F/gas 6. Leaving the skin on, cut the potatoes into thick chips. Dry the potatoes well on kitchen paper, then coat them in a bowl with the olive oil before scattering over a large baking tray. Bake for 25 minutes, turn them over and scatter with the garlic slices. Continue to cook for a further 20–25 minutes until crisp and golden brown. Season with salt before serving.

- Once the chips have reached their last 10 minutes of cooking, heat a ridged griddle pan or frying pan until smoking. Brush the steaks with olive oil, seasoning on one side only with salt and pepper. Fry the steaks, seasoned-side down, for 2–3 minutes before seasoning again, turning, and frying for a further 2–3 minutes for medium rare. Remove the steaks from the pan and allow to rest for a few minutes before serving with the garlic chips.

steak au poivre burger

serves **four**

1 large onion,
 finely chopped
1 egg
675g (1½lb) lean
 minced beef
salt and pepper
oil, for cooking
a knob of butter
2 tablespoons green
 peppercorns,
 lightly crushed
2–3 slugs of brandy
1 teaspoon Dijon mustard
150ml (5fl oz)
 whipping cream
a squeeze of lemon

When cooking burgers, they should be treated as respectfully as fillet steak. With that in mind, I thought we'd serve these burgers just like steak. If the burgers are quite thick, an extra 1–2 minutes should be added for medium.

• Mix the onion and egg into the beef, seasoning with salt and pepper. Divide the mixture into four, shaping and pressing each into a burger.

• To cook the burgers, heat some oil and butter in a frying pan and once sizzling, cook them for 6–7 minutes on each side for medium. Remove from the pan and keep warm to one side.

• Pour off any excess fat and spoon in the green peppercorns. Add the brandy along with the mustard and cream. Simmer for a couple of minutes until the sauce has thickened and season with a pinch of salt and a squeeze of lemon.

• Pour any juices from the burgers into the sauce and spoon over the top of the burgers to serve.

and more

A heaped teaspoon of chopped parsley can be added to the sauce or sprinkled on top.

These burgers are wonderful with mashed potatoes or a plate of fries.

sirloin steak with hot red wine and mustard vinaigrette

serves **two**

2 x 225–275g (8–10oz)
  sirloin steaks
3 tablespoons olive oil,
  plus extra for brushing
salt and pepper
a knob of butter
1 heaped tablespoon
  finely chopped shallots
2 tablespoons
  red wine vinegar
1 teaspoon Dijon mustard

• Heat a frying pan and brush each of the steaks with a little olive oil. Season the steaks with salt and pepper on one side only and place them, seasoned-side down, in the pan. Fry for a few minutes before adding the butter, seasoning, then turning the steaks and continuing to fry for a further 2–3 minutes for medium rare. Remove from the pan and leave to rest.

• Spoon the shallots into the frying pan, reducing the heat slightly. Stir for a minute or two, pour in the vinegar and simmer until almost dry. Stir in the mustard and olive oil.

• Pour any juices released from the steaks into the vinaigrette, then spoon the dressing over each steak and serve.

beef 'coq au vin' stew

serves **four**

900g (2lb) diced stewing
  or braising steak
salt and pepper
50g (2oz) butter
200g (7oz) cubes
  of pancetta
2 cloves of garlic, crushed
2 bay leaves
1 sprig of thyme
2 large carrots, sliced
20 button onions, peeled
225g (8oz) button
  mushrooms
2 tablespoons plain flour
1 tablespoon tomato purée
1 bottle of red wine
400ml (14fl oz) tin of beef
  consommé or stock
1 tablespoon
  chopped parsley

The classic coq au vin flavours of red wine, mushrooms, bacon and button onions all lend themselves to this beef stew, which looks like it has quite a frighteningly long list of ingredients, but actually requires little preparation.

- Preheat the oven to 170°C/325°F/gas 3. Season the beef with salt and pepper. Heat a large casserole dish with the butter and once sizzling, fry the beef and pancetta until well coloured. Add the garlic, bay leaves, thyme, carrots, button onions and mushrooms. Cook for 2–3 minutes, then sprinkle in the flour and the tomato purée.

- Stir until the meat is well coated before pouring in the red wine and the beef consommé. Bring to a simmer, skim, then cover with a lid. Cook in the oven for 2½ hours until the meat is tender.

- Season if necessary with salt and pepper, skim, then scatter over the parsley and serve.

ragù

serves **four**

100g (4oz) cubes
  of pancetta
25g (1oz) butter
1 large onion,
  finely chopped
1 large carrot,
  finely chopped
2 sticks of celery,
  finely chopped
500g (1lb 2oz)
  lean minced beef
salt and pepper
300ml (10fl oz) milk
300ml (10fl oz) red wine
400g (14oz) tin of
  chopped tomatoes
400ml (14fl oz) tin of
  beef consommé

A classic from northern Italy, *ragù* is the original Bolognese sauce served with pasta. This recipe sticks close to the original, needing a few hours of slow simmering for the beef to soften and flavours to blend.

• Heat a large saucepan over a medium heat. Add the pancetta and fry for a few minutes until golden brown, then remove from the pan and keep to one side.

• Add the butter along with the chopped vegetables and cook over a low heat for 10–15 minutes. Season the beef with salt and pepper and add to the vegetables, increasing the heat and cooking the beef until brown. Pour in the milk and cook until well absorbed before adding the red wine. Bring to the boil and simmer until just half the liquid is left.

• Add the pancetta, tomatoes and half the consommé and return to a simmer. Cover with a lid and cook over a low heat for 2 hours, stirring occasionally. Add the remaining consommé if needed and check the seasoning before serving.

No Butter
No milk
No peanuts

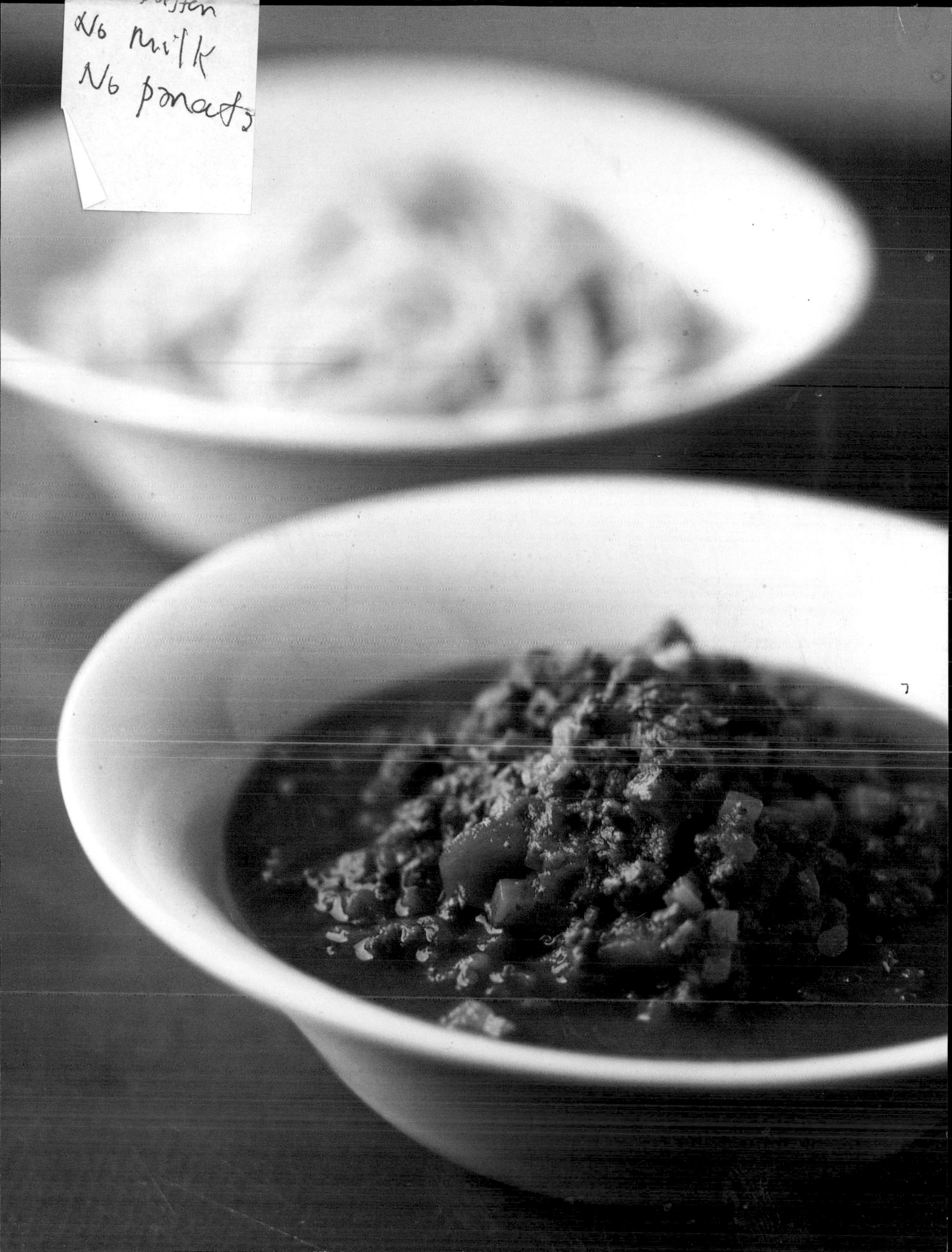

fillet of beef with goulash noodles

serves four

3 tomatoes
olive oil, for cooking
1 large onion,
  finely chopped
2 cloves of garlic, crushed
1 large red pepper, cut
  into small cubes
1 teaspoon paprika
300ml (10fl oz) passata
salt and pepper
350g (12oz) linguine
  or tagliatelle
2 knobs of butter
4 x 150–175g (5–6oz)
  beef fillet steaks
2 teaspoons
  chopped chives
4 tablespoons sour cream

With the point of a knife, remove the eye from the tomatoes. Place in a bowl, cover with boiling water and leave to stand for just 10–15 seconds before placing under cold running water. Peel away the skin, quarter the tomatoes, deseed and cut the flesh into cubes.

Heat a saucepan with some olive oil. Add the onion, garlic, pepper and paprika and stir over a medium heat for 6–7 minutes until they begin to soften. Pour the passata into the pan and bring to a gentle simmer. Allow the sauce to murmur softly for 10–15 minutes, adding the tomato during the final few minutes. Season with salt and pepper. Should the sauce become too thick, simply loosen with a few tablespoons of water.

Cook the pasta until tender, then drain, adding a drizzle of olive oil, a knob of butter and seasoning with salt and pepper.

Meanwhile, season the steaks with salt and pepper. Heat a frying pan with a bit more olive oil and, once hot, cook the steaks over a high heat for 3–4 minutes on each side for rare to medium rare. Add the remaining butter and, once sizzling, baste the steaks before removing from the pan. Leave to rest for 1–2 minutes before serving.

The noodles can be left plain with the sauce spooned on top or stirred into the sauce before serving with the steaks. Mix the chives into the sour cream and drop a spoonful on top of the pasta.

and more

The steaks can be dusted with paprika before cooking for a spicier taste.

beef and potatoes braised in guinness

serves **four**

olive oil, for cooking
3 large onions, sliced
4 x 175–225g (6–8oz)
  pieces of chuck steak
  or braising beef
flour, for dusting
salt and pepper
440ml (16fl oz) Guinness
1 tablespoon muscovado
  sugar
400ml (14fl oz) tin of beef
  consommé or stock
4 large potatoes, peeled
  and halved

Preheat the oven to 170ºC/325ºF/gas 3. Heat some olive oil in a large frying pan, add the onions and cook over a medium heat for a few minutes until tender and golden brown. Spoon the onions into a casserole dish.

Toss the beef in the flour and season with salt and pepper. Heat a little more oil in the frying pan and fry the steak until well coloured on all sides, then add to the dish.

Pour the Guinness into the hot frying pan, stir to lift the sticky juices from the base and sprinkle in the sugar. Add the consommé and simmer for a minute before pouring over the beef. Cover tightly with a lid and cook in the oven for 1½ hours. Add a little water if necessary to keep the meat covered.

Add the potatoes and continue to cook for a further 1–1½ hours until the potatoes have absorbed and thickened the sauce and the beef is soft and tender.

and more

Serve the beef and potatoes with any green vegetable, such as steamed spinach or buttery cabbage.

The sauce can be finished with chopped parsley.

roast rib of beef

serves **six–eight**

1 x 3-bone rib of beef
salt and pepper

Preheat the oven to 220°C/425°F/gas 7. Put the beef joint into a roasting tray and season liberally with salt and pepper. Roast in the oven for 15 minutes, then reduce the oven temperature to 190°C/375°F/gas 5. Continue to roast following the approximate cooking times stated below:

roasting times

rare–medium rare	15 minutes per 450g (1lb)
medium	20 minutes per 450g (1lb)
well done	25–30 minutes per 450g (1lb)

To check the beef is cooked, pierce a skewer into the centre of the meat, leave for a few seconds, then remove and touch under your bottom lip. If it feels cold, the beef is not cooked; if warm, it is medium-rare to medium and if hot, well done. Once cooked, remove the joint from the oven and roasting tray, cover with foil and leave to rest for at least 20–30 minutes.

The rib can now be carved with ease and served with Yorkshire puddings and gravy.

roast beef trimmings
yorkshire puddings

serves **six–eight**

225g (8oz) plain flour
salt
3 eggs
1 egg white
300–400ml (10–14fl oz)
  milk
oil or dripping, for cooking

This Yorkshire pudding batter can be prepared and refrigerated up to 24 hours in advance to guarantee well-risen puddings.

Sift the flour and a pinch of salt into a large bowl. Add the eggs and egg white and whisk in 300ml (10fl oz) of the milk to make a thick batter.

If the batter is rested, it may thicken. To loosen, simply whisk in some of the remaining milk.

Generously oil or grease 2 x 12-cup bun trays or 1 medium roasting tray, preferably non-stick. During the last 10 minutes of roasting the beef, place the trays in the oven to heat.

Once the beef is resting, return the oven temperature to 220°C/425°F/gas 7. Fill the trays with the batter until almost full and bake for 20–30 minutes. For very crispy puddings, cook for a further 5–10 minutes.

gravy

serves **six–eight**

1 tablespoon plain flour
600ml (1 pint) beef stock
salt and pepper

The gravy is very simple to prepare, although the thick roast gravy on page 221 also complements roast beef.

To make the gravy, pour off most of the fat from the roasting tray, leaving about a tablespoon. Heat the tray on the stove, add the flour and stir over a medium heat until the flour begins to brown.

Stir in the stock, bring to the boil, then reduce to a simmer for a few minutes. Season with salt and pepper if needed, adding any released juices from the joint.

wild mushroom and garlic cream

makes **400ml** (14fl oz)

2 glasses of white wine
1 large clove of garlic,
  crushed
300ml (10fl oz) chicken or
  beef stock
200ml (7fl oz) double or
  whipping cream
225g (8oz) wild, chestnut,
  flat or button
  mushrooms, sliced or
  quartered
salt and pepper
1 tablespoon chopped
  chives

This sauce is an alternative to gravy for roast beef or lamb, creating a completely different flavour for the dishes.

In a saucepan, boil together the wine and garlic until just a quarter of the liquid is left. Add the chicken stock, return to the boil and boil until just half the liquid is left. Pour in the cream and simmer for 10 minutes.

Add the mushrooms and gently simmer for a further 5 minutes until the mushrooms are tender. Season with salt and pepper. Add the chives to the sauce just before serving with the roast beef.

fish seafood poultry pork
lamb beef **vegetables**
pasta and rice eggs and
cheese desserts

some inspiration for a box of year-round vegetables

Potatoes. One of Britain's most-loved ingredients, potatoes are for me one of the most valuable foods we have, lending themselves to almost every one of our savoury dishes.

Mushrooms. Out of all the cultivated mushrooms, I particularly like chestnut mushrooms with their nutty flavour. From all the wild mushrooms, ceps and morels are regarded as the finest.

Carrots. Vegetables that add a sweet flavour and have the kind of pleasing taste that suits everyone. They are easy to cook, easy to prepare and they work in all styles of cooking.

Onions. The essential thing about onions is that their savoury flavour is an enhancer that lifts dishes.

If you have year-round vegetables try . . .

Onions baked in their skins. Baked in a medium oven until overcooked, onions give off an amazing aroma when cut open. They can be almost puréed with the back of a spoon and treated like a soft, warm pickle to go with cold or hot meats.

Meaty mushrooms with spinach and cheese. Large, flat mushrooms provide a base for a vegetarian dish. Fill with spinach, onions and grated cheese and grill until browned.

Caramelized baby onions with roast pork. Blanch peeled baby onions in boiling water for a couple of minutes, then drain and cool. Roast in a tray in a medium oven until tender, rolling in honey or sugar with balsamic vinegar at the end to caramelize them until soft, very sticky and sweet and sour. Serve with a simple roasted leg or belly of pork.

Crispy bacon and potato fry-up. You can make a whole meal out of potatoes by frying a few strips of bacon or chopped sausages with chunks of cooked potato until golden brown.

Poached egg and mushroom toasts. Stack a poached egg, fried mushrooms and bacon on thick crisp toast for a simple supper.

Carrots with a fresh herb mayonnaise. Serve raw or cooked carrots with a herb mayonnaise.

Gorgonzola baked potatoes. Scoop out baked potatoes, add spring onions, butter and crumbled creamy Gorgonzola and put back in the oven to melt. If you don't have Gorgonzola, you can switch to goat's cheese, Parmesan, Red Leicester or slices of Brie.

Lyonnaise potatoes. Fry onion slices in butter, add to some sautéed potatoes and scatter over chopped parsley.

cooking your potatoes

simply the best roast potatoes

If you want your potatoes really crispy, you need to preboil them so their fluffy edges can catch as they roast.

Before you start: Place the potatoes in a saucepan of cold salted water, bring to the boil and simmer for 6 minutes. Drain and leave to stand for 3 minutes in the colander, then shake gently to crumble the potato edges so they crisp up as they roast.

I use: A large roasting tray.

Cook: Preheat the oven to 200°C/400°F/gas 6. On top of the stove, heat the tray with 5mm (¼ inch) of oil or lard. Roll the potatoes lightly in some seasoned flour, shaking off any excess. Once the fat is hot, fry the potatoes in the oil until completely golden brown and sprinkle with salt. Roast for 30 minutes, then turn in the pan and roast for a further 30 minutes. For a really crispy finish, roast for an additional 30 minutes.

simply the best chips

Rather than fry the potatoes twice, I like to preboil them, which leaves the chips with a creamier texture and prevents too much oil being absorbed. You then need only a little oil in the frying pan.

Before you start: Cut the potatoes into 1cm (½ inch) thick slices, then cut each slice into sticks. Place the potatoes in a saucepan of gently simmering salted water and simmer for 4–6 minutes until just tender. Drain, then lay the chips on a clean cloth until cool to dry out.

I use: With this method, the lack of oil means you only need a frying pan.

Cook: In a frying pan, heat a few centimetres of oil to 180°C (350°F). To prevent a drop in the oil temperature, fry just a handful of chips at a time until crisp, golden brown. Remove and drain on kitchen paper, then season with salt before serving.

simply the best mash

My mash is made from Desirée or Maris Piper potatoes mashed with cold butter and warm milk or cream. Season with salt and ground white pepper (black pepper leaves vanilla seed-like dots in the mash). I never hold back on the amount of butter, it creates an almost silky finish.

I use: A potato masher, ricer, mouli-legume or sieve to mash the potatoes.

Cook: Cook the potatoes in a pan of boiling, salted water until tender. Drain well, replace the lid and shake vigorously to break up the potatoes. Mash the potatoes, then add a generous amount of butter and a little milk or cream, a bit at a time, until the potatoes are soft, light and creamy. Season with salt and ground white pepper. For a slightly spicy edge, add some freshly grated nutmeg.

simply the best sauté potatoes

Any variety of potato can be used for sautéing. Potatoes with a waxy texture maintain their shape, while floury-textured ones tend to break up and crumble crisply when fried. Halved new potatoes also sauté very well.

I use: A non-stick frying pan.

Cook: Cook the potatoes in their skins in boiling salted water for 20 minutes until tender. Peel and cut into 1cm (½ inch) thick slices. Heat the frying pan, adding a little oil. Place a layer of potatoes in the pan and fry until golden brown, then turn and brown the other side. Stir in a large knob of butter and season with salt and pepper.

cherry tomato soup

serves **four–six**

olive oil, for cooking
2 red onions, sliced
2 cloves of garlic, crushed
2 tablespoons red wine
  vinegar
500g (1lb 2oz) cherry
  tomatoes, halved
300ml (10fl oz) passata
450ml (16fl oz) vegetable
  stock
coarse sea salt and
  pepper

- Heat some olive oil in a large, deep frying pan. Add the red onion and garlic and fry over a medium heat until softened and lightly coloured. Spoon in the red wine vinegar and allow it to boil until very little of the liquid is left.

- Add the cherry tomatoes and continue to fry for 10 minutes.

- Pour in the passata and stock, bring to a simmer and gently cook for a further 10 minutes.

- Finish with a sprinkling of sea salt and a twist of pepper.

and more

Torn fresh basil leaves can be sprinkled over the top of the finished soup.

asparagus vichyssoise

Serves **four–six**

16 asparagus spears
25g (1oz) butter
1 onion, sliced
2 leeks, trimmed and
  shredded
2 potatoes, peeled and
  cut into cubes
900ml (1½ pints)
  vegetable stock
150ml (5fl oz) single cream
salt and pepper
freshly grated nutmeg

- Cut the tips of the asparagus into 4cm (1½ inch) lengths, slicing the remaining spears finely.

- Melt the butter in a large saucepan and add the onion, leek and potato. Stir and allow to bubble gently, then cover with a lid and cook for 10 minutes. Pour in the stock, replace the lid, bring to a simmer and cook for 20 minutes. Add just the sliced asparagus and the cream and simmer for a further 10 minutes until all the vegetables are tender.

- Season with the salt and pepper and a little nutmeg. Liquidize the soup in a blender or food processor until smooth and pour into a bowl. Allow to cool before refrigerating to chill.

- Cook the asparagus tips in a pan of boiling salted water for several minutes until tender, then plunge into iced water. Once cold, dry on kitchen paper.

- To serve, divide the soup among the bowls and scatter with the asparagus tips.

and more

Half the cream can be saved and used to drizzle over the soup just before serving.

butternut squash soup with fresh herb croutons

serves **four**

4 tablespoons olive oil
1 large onion, sliced
1 clove of garlic, crushed
675g (1½lb) butternut
    squash, peeled,
    deseeded and cut into
    cubes
¼ teaspoon ground ginger
600ml (1 pint) vegetable
    stock
100ml (3½fl oz) orange
    juice
salt and pepper
2–3 slices of thick white
    bread, crusts removed
    and cut into cubes
a knob of butter
2 teaspoons chopped
    mixed herbs (chives,
    parsley, chervil)
6 tablespoons single
    cream, crème fraîche or
    natural yoghurt

- Warm half the olive oil in a large saucepan and add the onion and garlic. Cook over a low heat until soft but without colour. Add the butternut and the ginger and gently cook for 5 minutes. Add the vegetable stock and the orange juice and simmer for 20–30 minutes until the butternut is tender.

- Purée the soup in a blender or food processor until smooth and season with salt and pepper. Return the soup to a clean pan, ready to warm through when needed.

- To make the croutons, heat the remaining olive oil in a frying pan and once hot, scatter in the bread and fry until all the sides are golden brown. Season with a pinch of salt, then add the knob of butter and herbs.

- To serve, stir the cream into the hot soup or drizzle in swirls on top and offer the crispy croutons separately or scatter them over.

and more

The orange juice can be replaced with milk for a more classic flavour.

Grated Parmesan sprinkled over the soup and croutons offer an Italian edge.

three bean salad

serves **six** as a starter or
 four as a main course

175g (6oz) fine
 French beans
175g (6oz) runner beans
400g (14oz) tin of
 cannellini beans, drained
100ml (3½fl oz) low-fat
 crème fraîche
½ teaspoon Dijon mustard
1 teaspoon sherry vinegar
salt and pepper
2 tablespoons pine nuts
225g (8oz) mixed
 salad leaves
2 large shallots,
 sliced into rings
olive oil, for drizzling

French beans, runner beans and cannellini beans are the three featured in this recipe. The cannellini beans (Italian haricot beans) also help flavour the dressing.

- Trim only the tops from the French beans. Top and tail the runner beans, removing the side strings. At an angle, slice the runner beans into thin strips.

- Put 50g (2oz) of the cannellini beans, the crème fraîche, mustard and sherry vinegar into a blender or food processor and blend to a smooth paste. The dressing should be of a coating consistency. Season with salt and pepper.

- Preheat the grill. Spread the pine nuts on a baking tray and toast until golden in colour.

- Plunge the runner and French beans into a large saucepan of boiling salted water. Cook for a few minutes until tender, but with a slight bite. Drain the beans and leave to cool until just warm.

- Put the salad leaves and shallot rings into a large bowl, add the remaining cannellini beans and the warm beans and season with salt and pepper. Divide the salad among the plates, spoon the cannellini bean dressing over each and sprinkle with the toasted pine nuts. Drizzle with the olive oil before serving.

and more

Many other flavours can be added to the salad, with peppers and tomatoes working particularly well with the dressing.

Serve with slices of toasted ciabatta or French bread spread with garlic butter.

ratatouille omelette

serves **four**

50ml (2fl oz) olive oil, plus
  extra for drizzling
25g (1oz) butter
2 red peppers,
  cut into strips
1 green pepper,
  cut into strips
1 yellow pepper,
  cut into strips
1 small aubergine or half a
  large, cut into cubes
1 large courgette, halved
  and cut into thick pieces
1 clove of garlic, crushed
4 spring onions, sliced
salt and pepper
10 beaten eggs
75g (3oz) Pecorino cheese

- Heat the olive oil and butter in a large deep frying pan. Add the peppers, aubergine, courgette and garlic and stir over a high heat until they begin to colour. Reduce the heat slightly and continue to cook for a further 10–12 minutes until all are tender. Add the spring onions and season with salt and pepper.

- Over a low heat, pour the beaten eggs into the ratatouille and stir gently for 1–2 minutes, allowing the omelette to set and brown on the base.

- Preheat the grill. Sprinkle the grated Pecorino cheese over the omelette and melt under the grill. Drizzle with olive oil and serve in wedges, hot, warm or cold.

roast squash, beetroot and goat's cheese salad

serves **four**

1 butternut squash
6 tablespoons olive oil
salt and pepper
1 teaspoon grated
  orange zest
juice of 1 orange
1 teaspoon sugar
1 tablespoon
  wholegrain mustard
2 tablespoons
  red wine vinegar
4 cooked beetroots
225g (8oz) goat's cheese,
  at room temperature
100g (4oz)
  mixed salad leaves
50–100g (2–4oz) rocket
a handful of mixed fresh
  herbs (sprigs of chervil,
  flat-leaf parsley, chives)
100ml (3½fl oz)
  natural yoghurt

Goat's cheeses can be found in many shapes and sizes. It's best to choose small, smooth-textured cheeses, particularly rindless ones, which will blend very well in this salad and require virtually no preparation.

• Preheat the oven to 200°C/400°F/gas 6. Cut the squash in half lengthways and scoop out and discard the seeds. Halve each piece across the middle, cutting the quarters into small wedges. Arrange the pieces on a baking tray, drizzle with 2 tablespoons of the oil and season with salt and pepper. Roast for 40–50 minutes until tender and rich in colour.

• Meanwhile, boil together the orange zest, juice and sugar for 1–2 minutes until just a third of the liquid is left. In a small bowl, stir the orange juice liquid together with the mustard and red wine vinegar, whisk in the remaining olive oil and season with salt and pepper. Cut each of the beetroots into six wedges.

• To assemble the salad, spoon the beetroot, squash and broken pieces of the goat's cheese on to a large platter. Mix together the salad leaves, rocket and herbs and shake a little of the dressing through the leaves before scattering them over the top of the vegetables. The remainder of the dressing, along with the yoghurt, can be trickled over the top.

and more

The butternut squash can be peeled before using.

Orange segments can be included for a fruitier taste.

Equal quantities of walnut and groundnut oil may be used in place of the olive oil for the dressing.

pizza tomato tart

serves **two–four**

225g (8oz) ready-rolled
  puff pastry, frozen
  or fresh
3 tablespoons olive oil
2 onions, sliced
1 small clove of
  garlic, crushed
coarse sea salt
  and pepper
8–10 plum tomatoes
6–8 stoned black
  olives, halved
1 teaspoon
  balsamic vinegar

• Grease a large baking tray. Place the pastry on the tray before cutting into a rough 30cm (12 inch) disc, discarding the trimmings. Using a fork, prick the pastry disc all over and refrigerate for 20 minutes.

• Preheat the oven to 230°C/450°F/gas 8. Heat a tablespoon of the oil in a frying pan. Once hot, fry the onion and garlic together for a few minutes until they begin to colour and soften. Season with salt and pepper, remove from the pan and leave to cool.

• Halve the tomatoes lengthways. Sprinkle the onions over the pastry and place the tomatoes on top, flat-side up. Scatter over the black olives and season with the sea salt and a twist of pepper. Bake the tart in the oven for 20–25 minutes until the pastry is crispy and the tomatoes softened with a golden brown tinge.

• Brush the pastry border with a little olive oil, then mix the remaining oil with the balsamic vinegar and season with salt and pepper. Drizzle it over the tart before serving.

and more

Grated mozzarella and/or Parmesan can be sprinkled over the tart during the final 5 minutes of baking.

Torn basil leaves can also be scattered over the cooked tart.

asparagus and mushroom pudding with melting fontina

serves **four**

350g (12oz)
  small new potatoes
12 asparagus
  spears, halved
a large knob of butter
450g (1lb) mixed wild or
  chestnut mushrooms,
  quartered if large
salt and pepper
4 eggs
25g (1oz) plain flour
200ml (7fl oz)
  crème fraîche
50ml (2fl oz) milk
1 teaspoon thyme leaves
100g (4oz)
  Fontina cheese,
  rind removed and
  cheese cut into cubes
hazelnut or walnut oil,
  for drizzling (optional)

The 'pudding' is a savoury batter that encases the vegetables as they bake. Fontina is an Italian cow's milk cheese that has a delicate nutty flavour. Once melted it becomes earthier with a hint of mushroom.

- Cook the new potatoes in boiling salted water for approximately 20 minutes until cooked through. When cool, cut in half.

- Preheat the oven to 190°C/375°F/gas 5. Snap the woody end from each asparagus spear, cut the spears in half and drop into a large pan of boiling salted water, cooking for several minutes until tender. Plunge into iced water and dry on kitchen paper.

- Heat the butter in a large frying pan and once sizzling, add the mushrooms, turning them in the pan quickly before draining and leaving to cool. Mix the asparagus, mushrooms and new potatoes in a 23cm (9 inch) buttered flan or earthenware dish and season with salt and pepper.

- Crack the eggs into a food processor and blend with the flour, crème fraîche, milk, thyme and a pinch of salt and pepper until smooth.

- Pour the mix over the vegetables and bake for 35–40 minutes until golden brown and just set. During the last 5–10 minutes of cooking, scatter the Fontina cheese over the top to melt. Leave to rest for 5 minutes, drizzling with a little hazelnut or walnut oil if using.

potatoes stuffed with stilton, leek and mushrooms

serves **four**

coarse sea salt and
  pepper
4 large baking potatoes
50g (2oz) butter, plus an
  extra knob
100g (4oz) button
  mushrooms, quartered
1 large leek, sliced
100g (4oz) cream cheese,
  at room temperature
100–175g (4–6oz)
  Stilton cheese

- Heat the oven to 200°C/400°F/gas 6. Lightly sprinkle the sea salt over a baking tray, prick the potatoes and place on top. Bake for 1¼–1½ hours until cooked through.

- Meanwhile, melt the knob of butter in a large pan and once sizzling, add the mushrooms and fry for 1–2 minutes until they begin to soften and colour. Stir in the leek and continue to cook for a further 2 minutes until tender, then season with salt and pepper.

- Halve the cooked potatoes, scooping out the flesh into a bowl and saving the skins. Fork lightly to a crumbly texture and season with salt and pepper. Stir in the remaining butter and the cream cheese before folding in the leek and the mushrooms.

- Fill the skins with the mixture, place the potatoes back on the tray and crumble the Stilton over the top. Bake in the oven just until the cheese has melted.

and more

It is not essential to use Stilton; there are so many blue cheeses and Gorgonzola works particularly well. As an alternative to blue cheese, try grated Cheddar or Gruyère.

parsnip cream

serves **four**

900g (2lb) parsnips
milk, to cover
a knob of butter
salt and pepper

This purée can be left quite thick or loosened with more milk to a sauce consistency. It is particularly delicious served with lamb.

- Peel the parsnips, cut each lengthways and remove the core before cutting into cubes.

- Place the parsnips in a saucepan and add enough milk to cover.

- Cover with a lid and simmer for 15–20 minutes until tender. Using a slotted spoon, transfer the parsnips to a food processor and blitz to a smooth texture, adding a little of the milk to loosen if needed.

- Stir in the butter and season with salt and pepper.

and more

As with all vegetable purées, it's best to use ground white pepper for the smoothest of finishes.

pumpkin with lime yoghurt

serves **four**

900g (2lb) pumpkin
olive oil, for drizzling
coarse sea salt and
  pepper
25g (1oz) butter
150ml (5fl oz) natural
  yoghurt
juice of 1 lime
1 tablespoon chopped
  flat-leaf parsley

- Preheat the oven to 190°C/375°F/gas 5. Leaving the skin on, cut the pumpkin wedges, removing the seeds and stringy pith.

- Place the pumpkin in a roasting tray, drizzle with the olive oil and season with salt and pepper. Roast for 1¼ hours until tender and golden brown. Add the butter to the tray, spooning it over the pumpkin as it melts.

- Whisk together the yoghurt, lime juice and parsley. Place the pumpkin in a serving dish and drizzle over the yoghurt or offer it separately.

mixed roast

serves **four**

3 tablespoons oil
4 carrots
4 parsnips
4 small onions
1 swede, quartered
salt and pepper
a large knob of butter

- Preheat the oven to 180°C/350°F/gas 4. Pour the oil into a roasting tray, scatter and roll the vegetables in the oil and season with salt and pepper.

- Roast the vegetables for 50–60 minutes, turning occasionally, until tender and golden brown. Brush with butter before serving.

baked potatoes with sour cream, chives and bacon

serves **four**

4 baking potatoes
coarse sea salt and
 pepper
100g (4oz) cubes of
 pancetta or bacon
4 tablespoons sour cream
handful of chopped chives

To guarantee a crisp-skinned and fluffy-textured baked potato, a floury rather than starchy variety of potato is the best choice. Should you prefer the skins to be softer, wrap the potatoes in foil.

• Preheat the oven to 220°C/425°F/gas 7. Prick the potatoes to release the steam created during baking. Scatter sea salt on a baking tray to prevent the skins from burning, place the potatoes on the sea salt and bake in the middle of the oven for 1–1½ hours.

• To make the croutons, fry the streaky bacon in a dry frying pan until coloured, then reduce the heat and continue to cook until crispy and crunchy. Dry the bacon pieces on kitchen paper.

• To serve, cut a cross in the top of each potato. Using a clean cloth, squeeze from the base so the four quarters open. Top with a spoonful of sour cream, a scattering of chives and the bacon croutons.

clapshot

serves **four**

450g (1lb) potatoes,
  peeled
450g (1lb) swedes, peeled
75g (3oz) butter
salt and pepper
a generous pinch of
  freshly grated nutmeg

Equal quantities of potato and swede, or turnips the nearer to Scotland you are, cooked and mashed together with lots of butter. Usually served smooth, I prefer to just crush them with a fork.

• Quarter the potatoes and cut the swedes into similar-sized pieces. Simmer the two together in a pan of boiling salted water for 20–30 minutes until tender.

• Drain, then return to the pan and shake over a low heat for a moment to dry them out.

• Using a fork or potato masher, break the potato and swede up, leaving them as coarse or as smooth as you wish. Add 50g (2oz) of the butter and fork it through with salt, pepper and the nutmeg. The clapshot is ready to serve in a large bowl topped with the remaining butter.

and more

You can quickly fry thinly sliced spring onions in the butter to drizzle over the clapshot.

orange curd carrots

serves **four**

675g (1½lb) carrots, sliced
2 heaped tablespoons
  orange curd
salt and pepper

Orange curd rolled around cooked carrots leaves not only a glossy shine but a piquant sweet orange bite. These carrots work particularly well with the slow-cooked red wine lamb shanks on page 199.

• Cook the carrots in boiling salted water until tender. Once cooked, drain off the water, leaving about 2 tablespoons in the pan. Gently stir in the orange curd until completely melted, glazing every slice, and season with salt and a twist of pepper.

gratin dauphinois

serves **four–six**

5 potatoes
500ml (18fl oz) double or
  whipping cream
salt and pepper
freshly grated nutmeg
1 clove of garlic, halved
butter, for greasing

- Preheat the oven to 150°C/300°F/gas 2. Peel and slice the potatoes thinly (preferably using a mandolin). Do not put the potatoes into water as this will remove the starch needed to thicken the cream.

- Place the slices in a bowl, pour in the cream and season with salt, pepper and the nutmeg. Carefully mix all the flavours together without breaking up the potatoes.

- Rub the base and sides of an earthenware dish with the garlic clove halves, squeezing well to release the juices, and smear the dish with butter. Layer the creamy potatoes evenly and cover with buttered foil.

- Bake for 40 minutes, remove the foil and continue to bake for a further 20–30 minutes until golden and tender. Leave the potatoes to rest for 10–15 minutes before serving.

celeriac fries

serves **four–six**

2 large celeriacs
3 tablespoons olive oil
coarse sea salt and
  pepper

I like to serve these nutty chips with the roast rib of beef (see page 235) or beef with a green peppercorn sauce (see page 219) and a mixed or green salad. The fries can be roasted while resting the beef.

- Preheat the oven to 220°C/425°F/gas 7.

- Cut away the top and bottom of the celeriacs and trim off the surrounding coarse skin. Cut the celeriac into chunky chips.

- Pour the olive oil into a large roasting tray and heat in the oven for 5 minutes. Add the celeriac chips to the roasting tray, turn in the oil and season with the salt and pepper. Roast for 20–25 minutes until golden brown.

savoy cabbage with shallots and parma ham

serves **four**

1 small savoy cabbage
50g (2oz) butter
100g (4oz) shallots, sliced
  into rings
6 slices of Parma ham, cut
  into squares
salt and pepper

- Remove the tough loose outside leaves from the cabbage. Cut the cabbage into quarters and remove the white core. Cut each piece into squares.

- Melt half the butter in a large pan and, once sizzling, add the shallot rings and cook until they begin to soften and lightly colour. Add the Parma ham squares and continue to cook for a further few minutes.

- Meanwhile, plunge the cabbage into a large pan of boiling salted water and cook for a few minutes until tender with a slight bite. Drain well.

- Add the cabbage to the shallots and ham with the remaining butter and season with salt and pepper.

pear red cabbage

serves **four–six**

1 small red cabbage or
  half a large, thinly sliced
3 pears, peeled, cored
  and cut into cubes
1 large onion, sliced
300ml (10fl oz) red wine
2 tablespoons honey
a knob of butter
200ml (7fl oz) sloe gin
salt and pepper

I've included sloe gin in this recipe. Sloe berries are the fruit of the blackthorn, small and blue-black, and their flavour blends wonderfully with gin. If you don't have any sloe gin, replace with an extra 200ml (7fl oz) red wine.

- Preheat the oven to 170°C/325°F/gas 3. Put all the ingredients into a braising pot with 150ml (5fl oz) of the sloe gin and season with salt and pepper. Bring to a simmer, cover with parchment paper and a lid and cook in the oven for 2 hours until syrupy.

- Check the cabbage after 1–1½ hours and, if dry, add a little water to moisten and continue braising.

- Once cooked, stir in the remaining sloe gin before serving.

and more

The blackcurrant liqueur *crème de cassis* can also be used in place of the sloe gin.

brussels sprouts rolled in chestnut cream

serves **four**

675g (1½lb) Brussels
 sprouts
100ml (3½fl oz) whipping
 cream
3 tablespoons
 unsweetened chestnut
 purée
salt and pepper

- Remove any loose or damaged outside leaves from the sprouts and cut a small cross into each base. Plunge the sprouts into a deep pan of boiling salted water and cook for 2–4 minutes until tender with a crisp bite, then drain.

- Meanwhile, warm the cream and chestnut purée in a frying pan, whisking together, then add the cooked sprouts and roll in the cream until all are coated. Season with salt and pepper and serve.

spicy cauliflower

serves **four**

1 small cauliflower, divided
  into florets
oil, for cooking
1 large onion, sliced
1 clove of garlic, crushed
1 teaspoon medium curry
  powder
a knob of butter
salt and pepper
1 tablespoon chopped
  coriander
150ml (5fl oz) natural
  yoghurt
a generous squeeze
  of lime

• Plunge the cauliflower into a pan of boiling salted water and cook for a few minutes until tender before draining.

• Heat the oil in a wok or frying pan. Add the onion, garlic and curry powder and fry for 5–6 minutes over a medium heat. Add the knob of butter and cauliflower and continue to fry for a further 5 minutes, stirring to coat the florets with the curry flavour. Season with a pinch of salt and sprinkle with the coriander.

• While the cauliflower is cooking, mix together the yoghurt with the lime juice and season with the salt and pepper. Drizzle the yoghurt over the cauliflower just before serving or offer separately.

broccoli with caesar dressing

serves **four–six**

50ml (2fl oz) mayonnaise
100ml (3½fl oz) crème
  fraîche
1 small clove of garlic,
  crushed
1 teaspoon Dijon mustard
1 teaspoon capers
1 tablespoon lemon juice
a dash of Tabasco
a dash of Worcester sauce
salt and pepper
900g (2lb) broccoli,
  divided into florets
25–50g (1–2oz) Parmesan
  cheese, grated or shaved

- Put the mayonnaise, crème fraîche, garlic, mustard, capers, lemon juice, Tabasco and Worcester sauces and a pinch of salt into a food processor or blender and blitz to a smooth purée.

- Drop the broccoli florets into a pan of boiling salted water and cook for 3–5 minutes until tender. Drain the florets, season with salt and pepper and arrange in a serving dish.

- Spoon the dressing over the broccoli and top with the Parmesan or offer separately.

runner beans with chunky seasoning

serves **four**

675g (1½lb) runner beans
25g (1oz) butter
1 tablespoon green
  peppercorns in brine,
  chopped
coarse sea salt

The chunky seasoning is coarse sea salt and green peppercorns, the two replacing the usual table salt and pepper.

• Top and tail the beans, pull away the strings from the sides and cut at an angle into thin strips. Plunge the beans into a pan of boiling salted water and cook for a few minutes until tender. Drain well.

• Melt the butter in a saucepan with the green peppercorns and, once sizzling, add the beans. Stir over a medium heat for 1–2 minutes, season with a sprinkling of sea salt and serve.

toasted sesame mangetout

serves **four**

1 heaped tablespoon
  sesame seeds
450g (1lb) mangetout
a large knob of butter
salt and pepper

- Fry the sesame seeds in a dry pan until toasted and golden brown, then remove from the pan to prevent further cooking.

- Snap the tops from the mangetout and plunge the mangetout into a pan of boiling salted water for 1 minute before draining.

- Melt the butter in a wok or frying pan. Once sizzling, add the mangetout, then the sesame seeds, and stir. Season with salt and pepper.

lemon and tarragon carrots

serves **four**

600g (1lb 5oz) carrots,
  peeled and sliced
25g (1oz) melted butter
1 teaspoon sugar
finely grated zest of
  ½ lemon
coarse sea salt and
  pepper
1 heaped teaspoon
  chopped tarragon
a squeeze of lemon

- Cook the carrots in a pan of boiling salted water until tender, then drain well and return to the pan.

- Meanwhile, mix together the butter, sugar and lemon zest. Stir the flavoured butter into the carrots, seasoning with salt and pepper. Finish with the tarragon and lemon juice.

fish seafood poultry pork lamb beef vegetables pasta and rice eggs and cheese desserts

turning simple braised rice into supper

Pilaffs, pilaus, pullaos and paellas are all braised rice dishes, but braised rice can just replace boiled rice as an accompaniment to a meal or, with the addition of other flavours, become the main course.

Try any of these additions:

Spices. Add spices to the butter at the start of cooking. A couple of cardamom pods, a cinnamon stick or some dry-roasted cumin or coriander seeds turn the braised rice into an aromatic spicy pilau rice.

Tomatoes. Stir in chopped ripe tomatoes at the end of the cooking.

Prawn skewers. Put 3–4 prawns on skewers, brush with butter, salt and pepper and heat under the grill for a few minutes on each side until cooked through. Serve with herby braised rice.

Nuts. Add cashew nuts, shelled pistachios or toasted pine nuts at the beginning of cooking, perhaps with some spices, for Eastern-flavoured rice.

Eggs. Stirring in a couple of eggs at the last moment, perhaps with some peas and chopped bacon, gives the rice an almost fried rice taste.

Grilled vegetables. Coat sliced courgettes, peppers or tomatoes with a little olive oil and grill until just browned. Pile on top of the braised rice.

Herbs. Add a handful of fresh chopped herbs at the end of the cooking time.

Spicy meatballs. Braised rice goes wonderfully with little minced pork meatballs, blended with an egg, some breadcrumbs and flavoured with Mediterranean herbs and Parmesan or chilli and coriander. Fry for a few minutes in oil and serve on top of the rice.

pasta carbonara

serves **four**

olive oil, for cooking
2 packets of sliced Parma
  ham, cut into 2cm
  (¾inch) squares
150ml (5fl oz) double cream
4 egg yolks
salt and pepper
400–500g (14–18oz) dried
  pasta
a squeeze of lemon
75g (3oz) Parmesan cheese

• Heat some olive oil in a large saucepan. Add the Parma ham squares and fry over a medium heat for a few minutes until the ham becomes crispy, then leave to one side.

• Mix together the cream and egg yolks and season with salt and pepper.

• Meanwhile, cook the pasta until tender. Drain, return it to the hot saucepan and stir in the lemon juice with the egg yolks and cream mixture. The heat from the pasta will partially cook the cream sauce.

• Check the seasoning and stir in the Parmesan and the Parma ham.

pasta with tomato, mozzarella and basil

serves **four**

8 tomatoes, quartered, deseeded and cut into chunky cubes
225g (8oz) mozzarella, cut into small cubes or grated
1 red onion, thinly sliced
1 small bunch of basil, torn
6 tablespoons olive oil
400–500g (14–18oz) dried pasta
coarse sea salt and pepper

This no-cook raw sauce can also be used as a simple side salad.

• In a large bowl, mix the tomato, mozzarella, red onion, basil and olive oil together.

• While making the sauce, cook the pasta until tender. Drain and add to the finished sauce. Season with sea salt and a twist of pepper.

fiery tomato sauce

serves **four**

olive oil, for cooking
2 onions, finely chopped
2 cloves of garlic, crushed
a pinch of dried oregano
2 red peppers
2 red chillies, deseeded
 and sliced into rings
4 plum tomatoes
400g (14oz) passata
salt and pepper
400–500g (14–18oz) dried
 pasta

- Warm the olive oil in a large deep frying pan, add the onions, garlic and oregano and cook gently until translucent.

- With a potato peeler, remove the skin from the red peppers and cut into 1cm (½ inch) cubes. Add the peppers and chillies to the onions and continue to cook for a further 6–8 minutes.

- With the point of a knife, remove the eyes from the tomatoes. Place in a bowl, cover with boiling water and leave to stand for 10–15 seconds before placing under cold running water. Peel away the skin, then quarter the tomatoes, deseed and cut the flesh into cubes.

- Add the tomato cubes to the sauce, increase the heat and cook until very little of the tomato juice is left. Pour the passata into the pan and bring to a simmer. Cook the sauce gently for 10 minutes and season with salt and pepper.

- While making the sauce, cook the pasta until tender. Drain and add to the finished sauce.

pasta niçoise

serves **four**

50g (2oz) fine French
 beans
200g (7oz) tin of tuna in
 oil, drained and flaked
225g (8oz) cherry
 tomatoes, quartered
10 black olives, stoned
 and quartered
4 spring onions, sliced
8 tablespoons olive oil
2 tablespoons
 tarragon vinegar
2 teaspoons Dijon mustard
1 clove of garlic, crushed
1 heaped teaspoon
 chopped tarragon
salt and pepper
400–500g (14–18oz) dried
 pasta

- Cook the French beans in a pan of boiling salted water for a few minutes until tender but still with a slight bite. Drain and place under cold running water. Cut the beans into 2cm (¾ inch) sticks.

- In a large bowl, mix together the beans, tuna flakes, cherry tomatoes, black olives and spring onions.

- Put the oil, vinegar, mustard, garlic, tarragon and some salt and pepper into a screw-top jar and give it a good shake.

- While making the sauce, cook the pasta until tender. Drain and add to the tuna. Pour over the dressing and stir together before serving

gorgonzola, parma ham and rocket sauce

serves **two**

50g (2oz) butter
100ml (3½fl oz)
  single cream
175g (6oz) Gorgonzola
  cheese, crumbled
50g (2oz) grated
  mozzarella
200–250g (7–9oz) dried
  pasta
1 large handful of
  rocket leaves
pepper
4 slices of Parma ham,
  torn into pieces
4 tablespoons walnut oil
  (optional)

- Warm the butter and single cream together in a pan, add the Gorgonzola and mozzarella and gently melt over a low heat.

- While making the sauce, cook the pasta until tender. Drain and add to the finished sauce with the rocket. Season with a twist of pepper and divide the pasta into bowls. Arrange the Parma ham on top.

- Drizzle with the walnut oil just before serving, if using.

and more

Extra single cream or crème fraîche can be added for a looser sauce.

bloody mary sauce

serves **four**

a large knob of butter
1 onion, finely chopped
3 tomatoes
500g (1lb 2oz) passata
a squeeze of lemon
1 teaspoon
  Worcester sauce
a dash of Tabasco
a pinch of celery salt
pepper
400–500g (14–18oz) dried
  pasta
a splash of vodka

This recipe adopts the flavours of the classic tomato-based vodka cocktail, but the vodka is optional. The pasta can also be served with grilled meats, particularly lamb chops or cutlets and chicken breasts.

• Melt the butter in a saucepan and gently fry the onion until soft.

• With the point of a knife, remove the eyes from the tomatoes. Place in a bowl, cover with boiling water and leave to stand for 10–15 seconds before placing under cold running water. Peel away the skin, then quarter the tomatoes, deseed and cut the flesh into cubes.

• Add the passata and tomato cubes to the onions, simmer and cook for 5 minutes. Add the lemon juice, Worcester sauce and the Tabasco. Season with the celery salt and a twist of pepper, finishing with a splash of vodka.

• While making the sauce, cook the pasta until tender. Drain and add to the finished sauce.

lemon and chive sauce

serves **four**

2 tablespoons olive oil
finely grated zest and juice
 of 1 lemon
150ml (5fl oz) double or
 whipping cream
salt and pepper
2 heaped tablespoons
 chopped chives
400–500g (14–18oz) dried
 pasta
50g (2oz) grated
 Parmesan cheese

- Warm the olive oil in a saucepan, add the lemon zest and lemon juice and simmer gently for 1 minute. Add the cream, return to a simmer and cook for a further 2–3 minutes. Season with salt and pepper and stir in the chives.

- While making the sauce, cook the pasta until tender. Drain and add to the finished sauce. Stir in half the Parmesan and offer the remainder separately.

and more

Possible additions are prawns, crabmeat, tinned tuna flakes, quickly fried cubes of chicken, broccoli florets, chopped mixed fresh herbs (parsley, chervil) or peas.

pasta tartare

serves **four**

1 heaped tablespoon
  chopped capers
1 heaped tablespoon
  finely chopped gherkins
1 bunch of spring
  onions, sliced
125ml (4fl oz) olive oil
juice of 1 lemon
400–500g (14–18oz) dried
  pasta
coarse sea salt and pepper
1 tablespoon
  chopped chives
1 tablespoon
  chopped parsley

This recipe suits any length, width or shape of pasta as a complete dish or as an accompaniment to fish or shellfish.

- Put the capers, gherkins, spring onions and olive oil into a deep frying pan, bring to a simmer and add the lemon juice.

- While making the sauce, cook the pasta until tender. Drain and add to the finished sauce. Season with the sea salt and a twist of black pepper and add the chives and parsley.

and more

Prawns, shrimps, crabmeat, lobster, tinned tuna, salmon, smoked salmon or smoked trout can all be added to the sauce.

A few spoonfuls of crème fraîche can also be stirred in.

pasta with chicken, sage and onion butter

serves **four**

olive oil, for cooking
2 large chicken breasts,
   skinless and sliced into
   thin strips
salt and pepper
2 large red onions, sliced
1 clove of garlic, crushed
100g (4oz) butter
1 small bunch of sage,
   leaves torn into pieces
400–500g (14–18oz) dried
   pasta

- Heat a large deep frying pan with the olive oil. Season the chicken strips with salt and pepper, add to the hot oil and fry over a high heat, turning once or twice.

- Add the red onions and garlic to the pan with a large knob of the butter and continue to fry for 5–6 minutes.

- Add the remaining butter and sage, seasoning with salt and pepper.

- While making the sauce, cook the pasta until tender. Drain and add to the finished sauce.

and more

100–150g (4–5oz) rindless Fontina cheese cubes or grated mozzarella work very well with this dish.

pasta with spinach and melting brie

serves **four**

a knob of butter
175g (6oz) baby spinach
salt and pepper
a pinch of freshly
  grated nutmeg
200ml (7fl oz) crème fraîche
400–500g (14–18oz) dried
  pasta
225g (8oz) Brie, very thinly
  sliced into lengths
olive oil, for drizzling

• Melt the butter in a large deep frying pan. Once sizzling, add the spinach leaves and turn in the pan for a minute until wilted. Season with the salt, pepper and nutmeg. Add the crème fraîche.

• While making the sauce, cook the pasta until tender. Drain and add to the finished sauce before checking the seasoning.

• Preheat the grill. Place the pasta in a large ovenproof dish and lay the Brie slices over the top. Place under the grill and warm the Brie until it melts into the pasta. Finish with a drizzle of olive oil and a twist of pepper.

wild mushroom cream sauce

serves **four**

25g (1oz) dried porcini or
 mixed wild mushrooms
a knob of butter
1 onion, finely chopped
1 glass of white wine
150ml (5fl oz) double cream
salt and pepper
a squeeze of lemon
400–500g (14–18oz) dried
 pasta
olive oil, for drizzling

• Soak the porcini mushrooms for 20–30 minutes in 300ml (10fl oz) warm water. Once softened, scoop the mushrooms from the water, squeezing any excess juices back into the bowl, and keep the mushroom-flavoured water to one side. Roughly chop the mushrooms.

• Melt the butter in a saucepan, add the onion and simmer for a few minutes until it begins to soften. Pour in the white wine and boil until almost dry.

• Add the mushroom water and the chopped mushrooms and boil until just a quarter of the liquid is left. Stir in the cream and simmer to a loose consistency. Season with salt and pepper and sharpen the sauce with the lemon juice.

• While making the sauce, cook the pasta until tender. Drain and add to the finished sauce. Drizzle each portion with olive oil.

and more

1 tablespoon of chopped flat-leaf parsley can be added to the sauce.

fish seafood poultry pork lamb beef vegetables pasta and rice eggs and cheese desserts

keeping eggs simple

If you have eggs and cheese, you always have a meal. Put some bread into the toaster, open your fridge, and you'll find almost any savoury ingredient can be put together with an egg or a handful of cheese to make the quickest of suppers.

cooking your eggs

Eggs have this thrifty image that you only need one or two to make a meal. But eggs aren't an expensive item, so go ahead and buy half a dozen for a supper for two.

simply the best fried eggs

Fry your eggs in butter, rather than oil, to get that nice little nutty edge to them.

I use: The size of the frying pan is important. The larger the pan, the more room the eggs have to spread, so use a smaller pan. A non-stick pan is preferable.

Cook: Heat a knob of butter in a frying pan over a medium–low heat until the butter begins to bubble but not burn. Crack in the eggs and fry for 30 seconds until the white begins to set, then begin to baste the yolk with the butter. Once cooked, lift out the eggs and pour the butter over.

My best fried egg supper: Something I enjoy is to place a fried egg on top of pan-fried spinach and mushrooms.

simply the best boiled eggs

This method of cooking treats the eggs like a sirloin steak, with timings for rare, medium and well done.

Before you start: It's always a good idea to cook eggs at room temperature. Eggs straight from the fridge can crack.

I use: If you want to boil a lot of eggs, make sure you have a large saucepan of rapidly boiling water, otherwise the temperature of the water will be reduced, making timings harder.

Cook: Carefully lower the eggs into water that is boiling, but not too rapidly, and place on the pan's bottom to prevent cracking. Once done, run quickly under water to stop the cooking.

How long: The following cooking times are for room-temperature eggs (add 30 seconds for cold), timed from the point they hit the water:

	medium	large
very soft	3½ minutes	4 minutes
soft	4½ minutes	5 minutes
medium	5½ minutes	6 minutes
hard	7 minutes	8 minutes
(but with a moist centre)		
well done	9 minutes	10 minutes

My best boiled egg supper: Instead of toasted soldiers, dip asparagus or purple sprouting broccoli into some soft-boiled eggs.

simply the best poached eggs

The eggs need to be as fresh as possible, otherwise the egg whites tend to spread on contact with the water. If you don't think your eggs are really fresh, add vinegar to the water to help set the whites.

Before you start: Always poach in deep water. The deep water makes the whites collect around the yolks and the eggs become quite bulbous as they travel to the bottom of the pan.

I use: A deep saucepan.

Cook: Crack the eggs into cups and whisk the vigorously simmering water in a circular motion. Pour each egg into the middle of the spinning water to pull and set the white around the yolk and poach for 3 minutes until the white has set but the yolk still has a runny, warm consistency. Lift the eggs out with a slotted spoon and drain on kitchen paper.

My best poached egg supper: Ham topped with melted Cheddar cheese and a poached egg to finish.

simply the best scrambled eggs

The secret of scrambled eggs is to always take them off the heat slightly underdone. They will continue to cook in the pan or even on the plate.

Before you start: You need at least a couple of large eggs per person. For the simplest eggs, cook them with just a knob of butter and season with salt and pepper. If you prefer a really soft, moist texture, you can add milk, cream or water, but it's best to add no more than a tablespoon per egg because too much liquid can leave a puddle of eggy cream.

I use: A saucepan or frying pan.

Cook: Beat the eggs to combine the yolks with the whites. Melt a large knob of butter in the pan and once bubbling but before it browns, pour in the eggs, seasoning them with salt and pepper. Turn and stir the eggs with a wooden spoon fairly vigorously, covering every corner of the pan. Once the eggs start to set and get lumpy, but still have a soft consistency, remove the pan from the stove.

My best scrambled egg supper: Serve scrambled eggs with roasted tomatoes and cubes of buffalo mozzarella beginning to melt into the eggs. Fresh herbs make a tasty addition.

keeping cheese simple

creating a cheese board

If you're lucky enough to have a local cheese shop or farmer's market, you'll discover a huge amount of cheeses now available, with many cheese shops an Aladdin's cave of flavours.

At the cheese counter:

Pick out a good mix. There are so many to choose from, and here I've listed a selection of some that are easily available.

Hard: Cheshire, Red Leicester, Farmhouse Cheddar, Double Gloucester, Lancashire or Wensleydale.

Blue: Stilton, an Irish Cashel Blue, Roquefort, Gorgonzola, Dolcelatte or a Lanark Blue from Scotland.

Semi-soft: The award-winning Irish Milleens, Chaumes or Reblochon.

Soft: French or Somerset Brie, Camembert, a soft British goat's cheese or French chèvre. You may also be lucky enough to find the double and triple cream cheeses – Chaource and Explorateur.

How many? Three or four is enough if your cheese board is going to be part of a meal, but of course the choice is yours. If you're a big fan of one cheese, then just have that cheese, perhaps with a special bread you've chosen and a favourite wine.

how to bring it all together

Remember to take your cheeses out of the fridge. Cheese is never at its soft, ripe best when chilled.

The French style of eating cheese is before the dessert to keep the savoury flavours going and to use up the red wine from the main course. The British way of eating cheese is after the dessert to finish off on a savoury note. Really, it's up to you which you prefer.

Cheese doesn't have to be served with bread or crackers. A cheese plate is fabulous with grapes and apples or a fresh herb salad. Try celery; dates with soft cheese for that toffee effect; or pears with blue cheese.

If you are having a variety, don't let them overpower each other. It makes sense to start with the milder flavours and build up towards the blue.

key flavours for cheese

Nuts. Try cracked walnuts and nutty breads, particularly those with a sweet raisin bite.

Tomatoes. Make a nice little cherry tomato salad to go with your cheese selection instead of using more obvious fruit ideas.

Avocado. An avocado salad works well with a harder cheese or a crumbly goat's cheese.

Leeks, spinach and broccoli. Very few vegetables can't partner cheese, but these green vegetables take on the flavour of blue cheeses particularly well.

Pickles. There are so many pickles that were just made for cheese. Look for fruit-based ones like date or pear, sweet pickled peppers or beetroot.

Fruit. Have a bowl of cherries with your cheeseboard or try fresh peaches with soft or cream cheese.

Olives. Simplicity itself – a slice of cheese with a bowl of olives.

Black pepper. Twist black pepper on to soft cheese and trickle over a good oil.

Polenta. Cheese is marvellous stirred into warm polenta or melted over.

Ham. Serve a selection of cooked and cured hams with a few cheeses.

some simple cheese suppers

Potato, pepper and cheese bake. If you've got leftover new potatoes, half an onion and a red pepper sitting in your fridge, fry together until golden. Crack in 6 eggs for a supper for 2–3, stir, then pop under the grill with any cheese you have scattered over the top. Supper is done when the cheese melts.

Cheese and herb dip. Mix crème fraîche with fresh herbs and a soft cheese and serve with spring onions or flavoured breads for dipping.

Tomato soup with Gruyère croutons. Cut slices of French bread and pop under the grill with a topping of grated Gruyère and Cheddar. Scatter Parmesan on at the end to make croutons to top a bought fresh tomato soup.

Cheese-board toast. Scatter walnut or raisin bread with a mixture of cheeses, such as little bits of Brie, Gruyère and a strong blue, and toast until bubbling. Eat your cheese-board toast with something very crisp, perhaps pieces of apple, grapes or a simple salad.

Soft cheese and herb roast chicken. Take a little bit of soft or blue cheese and mix it with a cooked chopped onion, a handful of breadcrumbs, some fresh herbs and seasoning and pop under the skin of a chicken before roasting. This stuffing can also be used to fill or top vegetables ready for baking with a drizzle of olive oil.

Stilton salad. Mix room-temperature Stilton with cubes of apple, grapes and celery and some croutons made from a nut or fruit bread to turn the whole cheese course into a starter.

Roquefort cream sauce with steak. Make an instant sauce for steak, green vegetables or a baked potato by liquidizing room-temperature Roquefort with crème fraîche, salt and pepper.

omelette

serves **one**

3 eggs
15g (½oz) butter
salt and pepper

French-style omelettes are best cooked until just set, leaving a soft centre and not allowing the outside to colour or become leathery.

- Break the eggs into a bowl and whisk together with a fork.

- Warm a 15cm (6 inch) non-stick omelette pan over a medium heat, add the butter and swirl around the pan to cover the base and the sides.

- Season the eggs with salt and pepper. Once the butter begins to foam, add the egg mixture and move the pan back and forth, stirring the eggs with the fork until a soft scrambled consistency is reached. Cover the base of the pan with the egg and leave until just set.

- Hold the pan at an angle, slide the omelette towards the edge and fold it in, then fold the other side over to create a cigar shape. Turn the omelette out on to a plate and serve.

and more

Various fillings, such as cheese, onion, ham, tomatoes and herbs, can be added to the omelette.

potato and onion frittata

serves **six**

3 large potatoes, peeled
  and cut into small cubes
olive oil, for cooking
2 onions, thinly sliced
salt and pepper
8 eggs
25g (1oz) butter

A frittata is a flat Italian omelette, closer to the Spanish tortilla than the folded French omelette. It should be cooked slowly to leave a moist rather than a runny texture. It also should not be refrigerated before eating because this oversets the omelette, spoiling the flavour and texture.

- Cook the potatoes in a pan of boiling salted water until tender, drain well and place in a bowl.

- Heat the oil in a 22–25cm (9–10 inch) non-stick frying pan. Once hot, fry the onion over a medium heat until completely softened and a light golden brown. Add to the potato and mix well. Season with salt and pepper.

- Beat the eggs together and season with salt and pepper. Add the potato and onion and mix well.

- Heat the butter in the pan and once it begins to foam, pour in the egg mixture, stirring with a spatula. Cook over the lowest possible heat, stirring for the first 1–2 minutes. The omelette can now be left to cook and set, leaving a slightly loose runny top.

- Preheat the grill. Place under the grill until the top has set or cover with a large plate, turn the pan over and slide the omelette back into the pan to fry for a further few minutes. The frittata is now ready to serve hot, warm or at room temperature.

and more

The omelette can be flavoured with endless additions, ranging from herbs, vegetables, seafood or meats to the popular Italian Parmesan. Whatever the choice, each ingredient should be cooked if necessary before making the omelette.

bacon and egg salad

serves **two**

50g (2oz) blue cheese
6 tablespoons low-fat
  crème fraîche
pepper
oil, for cooking
2–4 slices of Bayonne,
  Parma or Serrano ham
100g (4oz) mixed salad
  leaves
a large knob of butter
2 large eggs

Streaky bacon works well in this salad, but here I've chosen a cured ham, which crisps up very nicely. The dressing for the salad is flavoured with a blue cheese such as Roquefort, Gorgonzola, Dolcelatte or Stilton, but can be substituted with a soft goat's cheese if preferred.

- Crumble the blue cheese in a food processor and blend with the crème fraîche and a twist of pepper.

- Warm the oil in a frying pan and once hot, fry the slices of ham for a minute until crispy. Mix the salad leaves with the dressing, scatter them over the plates and top with the crispy ham.

- Add the butter to the frying pan and once foaming, crack the eggs into the pan and fry and baste with the butter until the white is set and the yolk soft. Place the eggs on top of the salad, drizzling any butter over the top.

scrambled egg mushroom muffins

serves **two–four**

2 muffins, halved
25g (1oz) butter, plus extra
  for spreading
100g (4oz) mushrooms,
  sliced or quartered
6 eggs
2 tablespoons single
  cream or milk
salt and pepper
1 heaped teaspoon
  chopped chives
Parmesan cheese, for
  grating

- Preheat the grill. Brush each muffin half with butter and toast under the grill until golden brown.

- Melt half the butter in a frying pan and, once foaming, add the mushrooms and fry over a medium-hot heat for 1–2 minutes until softened. Spoon on top of the toasted muffins.

- Meanwhile, beat together the eggs and cream and season with salt and pepper. Melt the remaining butter in the frying pan and pour in the eggs, stirring continually with a wooden spoon until thick and creamy.

- Top the muffins with the scrambled eggs, sprinkle over the chives and grate Parmesan cheese on top of each one.

red leicester mushrooms

serves **six**

6 large flat mushrooms
salt and pepper
50g (2oz) butter
3 red onions, sliced
100g (4oz) Red Leicester,
  grated
50g (2oz) Gruyère or
  Emmental, grated
100ml (3½fl oz) double
  cream

Lightly butter a baking tray. Trim and discard the tip of the mushroom stalks and place on the tray, stalk-side up. Season with salt and pepper. Using half the butter, put small knobs on each of the mushrooms.

• Melt the remaining butter in a large deep frying pan and once sizzling, add the onions and fry over a medium–hot heat for 8–10 minutes until softened and lightly coloured. Season with salt and pepper.

• Meanwhile, preheat the grill and cook the mushrooms for 6–8 minutes until tender. Spoon the onions on top of the mushrooms.

• Mix the two cheeses in a bowl and stir in the cream. Top each of the onion mushrooms with the cheese mixture and return under the grill until the cheese has melted to a golden brown.

and more

A pinch of fresh marjoram or dried oregano can be added while cooking the onions.

macaroni and cauliflower with four cheeses

serves **four**

1 cauliflower, divided into
  small florets
350g (12oz) macaroni
350g (12oz) mixture of
  4 grated cheeses
  (Roquefort, Dolcelatte,
  Comté, Red Leicester,
  Emmental, Cheddar,
  Pecorino, Gruyère, Brie,
  Edam, Lancashire or
  raclette)
300ml (10fl oz) single or
  whipping cream
salt and pepper

- Cook the cauliflower and macaroni together in boiling salted water until tender.

- Meanwhile, mix together half of your chosen four-cheese mixture with the cream. Drain the macaroni and cauliflower well, stir into the cheese cream and season with salt and pepper.

- Preheat the grill. Place the macaroni in an ovenproof dish and sprinkle with the remaining cheese. Brown under the grill until the cheese is melted and bubbling.

and more

Finely shredded spring onion or chopped chives can be added to the cheese cream to give it an onion bite.

cheese fondue with toasted fingers

serves **four** as a snack

200ml (7fl oz) dry
  white wine
150g (5oz) Cheddar
  cheese, grated
150g (5oz) Caerphilly
  cheese, grated
½ teaspoon cornflour
1–2 teaspoons
  English mustard
a dash of Worcester sauce
pepper
ciabatta, focaccia, panini
  or any bread slices

The quantities listed here are enough for small snack bites, but double them if you are serving this as a complete starter

- Warm the wine in a saucepan over a medium-low heat to a gentle simmer. Mix the grated cheeses with the cornflour, stirring them little by little into the wine until completely melted and smooth. Do not boil the fondue because this will curdle the cheese. Remove the pan from the heat. Flavour the fondue with the mustard, Worcester sauce and a twist of pepper.

- Cut the bread into fingers and preheat the grill. Toast each slice to a golden brown.

- The fondue is ready to serve in a warm bowl along with the freshly toasted bread fingers.

and more

Both the mustard and the Worcester sauce can be omitted from the recipe to give a simple cheese fondue.

sweet and sour roquefort

serves **four** as a canapé

200g (7oz) Roquefort,
  crumbled
2 tablespoons sweet
  white wine
2 heaped tablespoons
  sour cream
pepper

Spoon into small tartlet cases or simply serve with cheese crackers. This picture shows these two recipes served as dips with the two spreads on page 356. (Clockwise from the back: goat's cheese and mango, sloe gin and Stilton, ouzo feta cream and sweet and sour Roquefort.)

• Beat the Roquefort with the white wine until smooth or blend in a food processor. Stir in the sour cream and season with a generous twist of pepper. Refrigerate until needed.

and more

The addition of chopped seedless grapes, placed under or on top of the mixture, helps to cut through the richness of the cheese. Chopped apple or celery also works very well.

ouzo feta cream

serves **four** as a canapé

300g (11 oz) feta cheese
pepper
3 tablespoons olive oil
1 tablespoon ouzo

This Greek-style cream would suit strips of pitta bread and is also ideal with crisp vegetable crudités, melted over hot new potatoes or spooned into a baked potato.

• To remove excess salt from the feta, soak in cold water or milk for 20–30 minutes.

• Remove the cheese from the water or milk and pat dry. Crumble into a food processor and add a generous twist of pepper. Blend the cheese and slowly add the olive oil and ouzo until you reach a smooth consistency. Refrigerate for 1–2 hours before serving.

hot potato salad with melting raclette

serves **four**

650g (1½lb) new potatoes
6 spring onions, thinly
  sliced
coarse sea salt and
  pepper
juice of 1 lemon
4 tablespoons olive oil
350g (12oz) raclette, rind
  removed and thinly sliced

Raclette is famous for its melting abilities and sweet, nutty flavour, particularly on potatoes. This salad can be served with hams, salamis, salads or pickles, but works equally well on its own or topped with a poached egg.

- Cook the new potatoes in boiling salted water for approximately 20 minutes until tender. Drain the potatoes well, cut each in half and scatter into an ovenproof dish. Sprinkle the spring onions on top and season with the salt and a twist of pepper.

- Preheat the grill. Mix the lemon juice with the olive oil and spoon over the potatoes. Arrange the raclette slices overlapping on top and place under the grill until the cheese has melted.

and more

A few spoonfuls of crème fraîche can be added to the potatoes before topping with the cheese.

If serving with a poached egg, a crisp green salad is a good accompaniment.

halloumi with cucumber pappardelle and avocado

serves **four** as a starter

1 cucumber
2 ripe avocados, peeled
  and cut into small cubes
5 tablespoons olive oil
juice of 1 lime
salt and pepper
1 tablespoon torn flat-leaf
  parsley
4 spring onions, sliced
  into rings
250g (9oz) halloumi
  cheese, cut into 4 slices

- Using a potato peeler, peel the skin and flesh of the cucumber in long strips into a bowl, discarding the soft seeded centre, and mix with the avocado. Whisk together 4 tablespoons of the olive oil and the lime juice and season with salt and pepper. Add the dressing to the salad with the parsley and spring onions.

- Place a non-stick frying pan over a medium heat. Once hot, add the remaining tablespoon of oil. Place the halloumi slices in the pan and fry for 1–2 minutes on each side until a rich golden brown in colour.

- Divide the salad among the plates and top each with a slice of the fried halloumi.

sloe gin and stilton bites

serves **four** as a canapé

olive oil, for cooking
1 small onion, finely
  chopped
3 tablespoons sloe gin
1 heaped tablespoon
  crème fraîche
175g (6oz) Stilton,
  at room temperature
1 tablespoon
  chopped parsley
pepper
1 stick of French bread,
  cut into 1cm (½ inch)
  thick slices
butter, for brushing

The combination of sloe gin and Stilton makes a very English flavour. For a more continental taste, replace the Stilton with Gorgonzola or Dolcelatte.

- Warm the olive oil in a small saucepan. Add the onion and cook for a few minutes until softened but without colouring. Add the sloe gin, increase the heat and cook until almost dry. Remove the pan from the heat and leave to cool slightly.

- Once the onions are just warm, spoon into a blender with the crème fraîche and crumble in the Stilton. Blend until smooth. Stir in the parsley and season with a twist of pepper.

- Preheat the grill. Toast the French bread slices on one side, then turn, brush the untoasted sides with butter and toast under the grill to finish. Spread or spoon the sloe gin and Stilton on top and serve.

goat's cheese mango spread

serves **four** as a canapé

100g (4oz) soft goat's
  cheese, rindless
2 tablespoons
  mango chutney
1 heaped teaspoon
  chopped chives
pepper

Perfect for warm toasts, small tartlet cases or on baked potatoes.

- Beat together the goat's cheese, mango chutney and chives. Season with pepper. The spread is now ready to use at room temperature or refrigerated.

cheddar cheese and onion scotch pancakes

serves **six–eight** as
  a starter

225g (8oz)
  self-raising flour
½ teaspoon salt
½ teaspoon mustard
  powder
2 eggs
150ml (5fl oz) milk
100g (4oz) mature
  Cheddar cheese, grated
1 large onion, grated
pepper
oil, for brushing

These pancakes make an easy vegetarian starter or savoury main dish served with a tomato salad. You can also drop the mixture into the pan in teaspoons to create snack bites.

- Sift the flour, salt and mustard powder together into a large bowl. Add the eggs and milk and whisk to make a smooth batter. Stir in the cheese, onion and a twist of pepper.

- Heat a large frying pan and brush with oil. Using a tablespoon, drop the batter into the pan in batches of five to six pancakes. Cook over a medium heat for 2–3 minutes before turning over and continuing to cook for a further 2 minutes. Place the pancakes inside a clean folded tea towel while frying the remainder of the batter.

and more

Cheshire cheese is a good variation to try in place of the Cheddar.

mozzarella and pesto potato cakes

serves **four**

4 large potatoes, peeled
  and quartered
salt and pepper
100g (4oz) mozzarella,
  diced
1 heaped tablespoon
  pesto
flour, for dusting
olive oil, for cooking

This recipe can also be made from leftover mash.

- Cook the potatoes in boiling salted water for approximately 20–25 minutes until completely tender. Drain and mash until smooth, seasoning with salt and pepper.

- Stir in the mozzarella and pesto and check the seasoning. Divide the mixture into eight, dust your hands liberally with flour and roll each piece into a ball. Lightly press on a floured surface into potato cakes.

- Heat 2 tablespoons of olive oil in a large frying pan and once hot, reduce the heat to medium and place the cakes in the pan without touching each other. Gently fry the cakes for 4–5 minutes until brown, turn and continue to fry for a further 3–4 minutes. The cakes can be kept warm in the oven while frying the remainder.

and more

It's not essential to make individual cakes; the mix can simply be pressed into a heated oiled frying pan, cooking as you would bubble and squeak. This could also be topped with extra cheese and melted under the grill.

leek, ham and brie slice

serves **four**

a large knob of butter
3 leeks, sliced
salt and pepper
375g (13oz) ready-rolled
  puff pastry
175g (6oz) piece of ham,
  cut into cubes
300–350g (10–12oz) Brie,
  cut into thin wedges
1 egg yolk
a splash of milk
olive oil, for drizzling

There are many soft-rind cheeses that can be used in place of the Brie. Try a Camembert or Coulommiers, a Sharpam from Devon or the Irish Cooleney.

- Melt the butter in a large saucepan and once sizzling, add the leeks and cook over a medium heat, without colouring, until they start to soften. Season with salt and pepper, then drain and leave to cool.

- Preheat the oven to 200°C/400°F/gas 6. Lightly brush a baking tray with oil, unroll the puff pastry and place on top. Using a fork, prick the base several times, leaving a clear 2cm (¾ inch) border around the outside.

- Add the ham to the leeks and spoon on to the pastry. Arrange the Brie wedges across the surface. Brush the pastry border with the egg yolk mixed with the milk.

- Bake in the oven for 20–25 minutes until the pastry is golden brown. Leave to cool slightly before drizzling with a little olive oil. Cut into slices to serve.

smoked haddock and spinach tart with emmental

serves **four–six**

225–275g (8–10oz) ready-made shortcrust or puff pastry
300g (11oz) fillet of smoked haddock, skinned
150ml (5fl oz) double or whipping cream
50ml (2fl oz) milk
225g (8oz) ready-prepared spinach leaves
100g (4oz) Emmental cheese, grated
2 eggs
1 egg yolk
pepper

- Preheat the oven to 200°C/400°F/gas 6. Lightly butter and flour a deep 20cm (8 inch) round tart tin and place on a baking tray. Roll out the dough on a lightly floured surface and line the tin, pressing into the sides and base. Any excess pastry above the top can be left overhanging. Refrigerate for 15 minutes before lining with greaseproof paper and filling with baking beans or rice. Bake for 15 minutes. Remove the greaseproof paper and baking beans and return to the oven for a further 5 minutes. Remove the pastry case from the oven, trimming around the top. Lower the oven temperature to 180°C/350°F/gas 4.

- Put the smoked haddock into a saucepan with the cream and milk. Bring to a simmer and cook for 4–5 minutes. Remove the fish from the pan and leave to cool slightly before separating into flakes. Keep the cooking cream to one side.

- Place the spinach in a large saucepan and cook over a medium heat until wilted. Drain and leave to cool in a colander.

- Sprinkle half the Emmental in the base of the pastry case, scatter the haddock flakes and spinach on top and finish with the remaining cheese. Whisk together the eggs, egg yolk, saved cream and a twist of pepper. Pour the mixture into the pastry case and bake for 30–35 minutes until the filling has just set. The quiche can be served warm or at room temperature.

and more

Single cream or all milk can be used in the filling for a lighter taste. Gruyère or Cheddar cheese can be used in place of the Emmental.

fish seafood poultry pork
lamb beef vegetables
pasta and rice eggs and
cheese desserts

keeping desserts simple

A really special dessert doesn't have to be an elaborate tart or rising soufflé; a ripe, sweet summer peach or warm poached fruit with chilled cream can make an irresistible end to a meal. The dessert recipes in this book are here just to give you some inspiration, so don't be afraid to change them. If you don't like a fruit or one of the accompaniments, go ahead and drop it to change the twist.

from the fruit bowl

The basic basket of dessert cooking is your fruit bowl. Bake your fruit to add sweetness or arrange on a fruit platter in the summer months to show off the particularly rich colours and flavours of all the berries and fruits available.

Apples. Make sticky baked apples filled with chopped marzipan and dried fruit.

Bananas. Roast bananas in their skins, open them up and trickle over golden syrup.

Blackcurrants and blueberries. Warm one or both of these berries in their juices with a spoonful of blackcurrant jam and a splash of sloe gin or kirsch to make a berry compote. Pour over a dessert or eat with ice cream.

Oranges, lemons and grapefruits. Citrus fruit segments provide a sharp contrast to hot pancakes sprinkled with sugar.

Peaches and nectarines. Bake soft fruits whole to retain their beautiful shape and juices and drizzle with a little golden syrup or honey.

Raspberries. Mix cream cheese with sugar and whipped cream and dollop it next to the wonderful late summer Scottish raspberries.

Strawberries. At their best raw or just gently softened with warm butter and brown sugar.

chocolate and nuts

Out of the summer months when fewer home-grown fruit are available, chocolate and nuts take on an even greater importance in dessert making. If you do love chocolate puddings, it doesn't mean you have to spend hours icing cakes; you can add a fabulous chocolate or nutty hint to a bought tart or fruit with any of these simple ideas.

Chocolate flakes. Grate a bar of chocolate over the top of a pudding or cake.

White or dark chocolate sauce. Melt any chocolate (white, dark or milk) and just pour over a dessert. For the richest of sauces, melt the chocolate with butter or cream.

Chocolate shavings. A garnish that adds texture as well as visual appeal to any chocolate dessert. Make the shavings by scraping a palette knife across a big block of room-temperature chocolate. Freeze until ready to serve.

Toasted nuts. Toast flaked almonds and scatter over baked fruit, toss with peach wedges in a hot wok to make a fruit stir-fry or use to top a tart with a dusting of icing sugar.

the finishing touches

If you want something special but really easy for dessert, follow the lead of the French and buy in a little treat from your local pâtisserie. Any of the following finishing touches will add a new dimension to the plate.

Ice cream. Buy in one of the many high-quality varieties now easily available. Stack up layers of ice cream, sliced bananas and grated chocolate to make little winter knickerbockers.

Citrus crème fraîche. Stir orange or lemon curd into crème fraîche and serve with a bought chocolate tart.

Strawberry sauce. Add a little strawberry jam to ripe, mashed strawberries to make a quick strawberry sauce.

Biscuits. Brandy snaps, sponge fingers, tuiles, cigarette biscuits or shortbreads all give an extra crispy texture to a soft dessert like an ice cream or mousse.

Icing sugar. Dust over a dessert for a professional finish.

Fresh mint. Finely chopped mint adds a fresh zing to any rich chocolate or fruit desserts.

Extra thick or clotted cream. Texturally these are a useful alternative to pouring cream and suit baked fruit particularly well.

Pre-made custard. Perk up a bought custard by adding a splash of liqueur and a spoon of whipped cream.

Fruit. Lift a bought tart with fresh fruit. Raspberries work really well, especially with a cheesecake, while raspberry jam loosened with water can give a nice glaze to a topping. Blackberries or pears are lovely with a bought tiramisu.

Sweet cream. Whip icing sugar into double cream or stir into really thick cream. Scraping in vanilla seeds turns this into a crème chantilly.

Vanilla sugar. Store a split vanilla pod in an airtight container of caster sugar for an aromatic vanilla-flavoured sugar to sprinkle over desserts and fruit.

Sprigs of berries. Sprigs of sharp black or red currants look beautiful draped over summer desserts.

Hot orange sauce. Sweeten the juice of an orange with marmalade, a little sugar, Grand Marnier or Cointreau. Serve with a steamed or chocolate sponge or pour over warm chocolate brownies.

some simple desserts

Pears with hot chocolate sauce. Bake halved pears in the oven, sprinkled with a little brown sugar to caramelize, until hot and soft. Serve with a rich chocolate sauce made by melting a bar of chopped dark chocolate, some single cream and a knob of butter in a bowl over simmering water.

Drunken summer fruits. Mix together a selection of red berries, dust liberally with icing sugar and drizzle equally liberally with crème de framboise (raspberry liqueur) or crème de cassis (blackcurrant liqueur).

Roast pineapple with Malibu custard cream. Roast chunks of pineapple with some butter and caster sugar in a medium oven until just softening, basting from time to time to almost caramelize. Mix together bought custard, whipped cream and a splash of Malibu and serve the chilled cream with the hot pineapple.

Raspberry or rhubarb fool. Combine crème fraîche, mascarpone and whipped cream with sugar and fold into puréed or mashed raspberries or a cooked rhubarb purée. Pour into glasses and top with fresh fruit or a trickle of cream.

Roasted figs with nutmeg. Roast halved figs, cut-side up, with a knob of butter, sprinkling of sugar and freshly grated nutmeg in a hot oven for about 15 minutes until soft. Serve with clotted cream.

Poached fruit plate. Arrange a fruit platter with the firmer fruits poached in a little water and sugar until just soft. Drizzle with a flavoured liqueur just before serving.

Iced mango soup. Purée a mango with orange juice and a grating of nutmeg. Freeze until ice cold, garnishing the finished soup with chunks of fresh mango, or perhaps papaya.

Cointreau oranges. Arrange slices of peeled orange neatly in a pudding basin and sprinkle generously with brown sugar and lots of Cointreau. Glaze under the hot grill and eat with an orange sorbet.

simple custards for desserts
fresh vanilla custard

makes **600ml** (1 pint)

200ml (7fl oz) milk
300ml (10fl oz) double
  cream
1 vanilla pod
50g (2oz) caster sugar
6 egg yolks

This fresh custard, crème anglaise, complements almost all desserts and puddings. It can be served warm or cold or even churned in an ice-cream machine for home-made vanilla ice cream.

- Pour the milk and cream into a saucepan. Split the vanilla pod in two lengthways and scrape the black seeds from each half with the point of a knife. Add the seeds and the pod halves to the milk and cream and bring to the boil.

- Meanwhile, whisk the sugar and egg yolks together in a bowl until thick, pale and creamy. Whisk half the boiled vanilla cream into the egg mixture, then pour the mixture back into the remaining cream in the pan. Cook over a gentle heat, stirring continuously, until the custard becomes thick and coats the back of a spoon.

- Remove from the heat and strain through a sieve into a jug or a bowl. Cover with clingfilm and leave to cool before refrigerating if serving cold. The custard can be kept in the refrigerator for up to 3 days.

chocolate brownie mousse

Serves **four**

225g (8oz) chocolate
  brownies, cut into cubes
225g (8oz) dark chocolate,
  chopped
300ml (10fl oz) double
  cream

This recipe is quick to make and resembles a chocolate trifle. Any bought chocolate brownies are fine to use and the mousse is best eaten at room temperature.

- Scatter the chocolate brownies in the base of a glass pudding bowl.

- Put the chopped chocolate into a bowl and place over a pan of simmering water, stirring occasionally until melted.

- Place half the cream in a pan and bring to the boil. Whisk into the melted chocolate until smooth and leave to cool slightly.

- Whip the remaining cream with a spoon until soft peaks form and fold into the chocolate, a little at a time. Pour the mousse over the chocolate brownies. The soft mousse is now ready to eat or can be refrigerated for 1–2 hours until firm.

and more

The mousse can be topped with grated chocolate, single cream or melted white, dark or milk chocolate poured over to give a neat, crisp topping.

Cherries from a tin or jar can be added to the brownies to create a Black Forest flavour, then drizzled with kirsch.

Rum, Grand Marnier or Kahlúa can also be added.

pink grapefruit posset

serves **six**

juice of 2 pink grapefruits
600ml (1 pint) double cream
175g (6oz) caster sugar
juice of 1 lemon

- Boil the grapefruit juice until just two-thirds of the liquid is left.
- Add the cream, sugar and lemon juice and simmer for 3 minutes.
- Leave to cool for a while, then pour the mixture into six glasses and refrigerate to set.

and more

A grapefruit and mint salad can be offered with the posset to enhance its flavour. To make, dust segments of grapefruit with icing sugar and sprinkle a few shredded mint leaves on top.

A teaspoon of grenadine added to the cream gives a rich pink colour.

Single cream can be poured over the posset before serving to soften this sweet, sharp dessert.

vanilla pear and peach salad

serves **four**

4 ripe pears, peeled,
  cored and cut into
  rough cubes
4 ripe peaches, stoned
  and cut into rough cubes
juice of 1 lemon or 2 limes
caster sugar, for sprinkling
1 vanilla pod, split and
  the seeds loosened

Seeds from the vanilla pod are used here to provide the spice flavour. If unavailable, simply replace with a splash or two of vanilla extract or essence.

• Place the fruit in a bowl with the lemon or lime juice and sprinkle over some caster sugar, depending on the ripeness of the fruit. Stir the vanilla seeds gently into the fruit, adding the scraped-out pods too.

• Refrigerate for 2–3 hours, stirring very gently just before serving.

and more

Serving with extra thick cream helps smooth the rich vanilla fruit flavour.

Fresh raspberries or strawberries work very well with this salad, sprinkled over the top just before serving.

baked apples with nutmeg custard pudding

serves **four**

600ml (1 pint)
  whipping cream
3 eggs
100g (4oz) caster sugar
freshly grated nutmeg
2 large dessert apples,
  cored and cut in half
  lengthways
1 tablespoon golden syrup
1 tablespoon light soft
  brown sugar
25g (1oz) butter

This dessert needs to be made several hours in advance. The nutmeg custard pudding is precooked and set before serving cold with the hot apples.

- Preheat the oven to 140°C/275°F/gas 1. Boil the cream in a small pan. Whisk together the eggs and sugar in a bowl and pour in the cream, whisking continuously. Pour the custard into an ovenproof dish and sprinkle liberally with nutmeg.

- Place in a deep tray and pour in boiling water from the kettle so it reaches halfway up the dish. Bake for 30–40 minutes until the custard is just set and has a slight quiver when gently shaken. Remove the pudding from the oven and tray and leave to cool. Refrigerate to chill.

- Preheat the oven again to 190°C/375°F/gas 5. Lightly grease a baking tray with butter and arrange the apple halves, cut-side up, on the tray. Spoon over the golden syrup and scatter on the brown sugar. Add a knob of butter on top of each apple half and bake for 15–20 minutes until tender.

- Divide the apples among the plates, spoon any syrup on top and accompany with a large spoonful of the nutmeg custard pudding.

and more

A tablespoon of Calvados can be mixed into the syrup for extra apple punch.

rice pudding with toasted honey plums

serves **four**

100g (4oz) short-grain
  pudding rice
900ml (1½ pints) milk
300ml (10fl oz) double
  cream
1–2 vanilla pods or
  a few drops of strong
  vanilla essence
50g (2oz) sugar
6 plums, halved and stoned
6 teaspoons honey

This rice pudding is good served hot or cold with the toasted plums.

• Put the rice into a sieve and pour over a full kettle of boiling water to rinse. Place the rice in a saucepan and add the milk and cream. Split the vanilla pods in half lengthways and scrape the seeds from the centre of each with the tip of a small knife. Add the seeds and pods to the saucepan.

• Bring the rice to the boil, then reduce the heat to a very gentle simmer and cook for 30 minutes, stirring from time to time to prevent the rice from sticking. Add the sugar and continue to cook for a further 10 minutes. Remove the vanilla pods.

• About 10–15 minutes before serving, preheat the grill and grease a baking tray with butter. Place the plum halves, cut-side up, on the tray. Drizzle a ½ teaspoon of the honey over each and cook under the grill, not too close to the heat, for 10–15 minutes until tender and golden brown. The plums can now be served with the rice.

apple jelly and cinnamon cream

serves **four**

300ml (10fl oz) sweet
  white wine
200ml (7fl oz) apple juice
100ml (3½fl oz) orange juice
juice of 1 small lemon
100g (3½oz) caster sugar
2 cloves
2 apples, coarsely chopped
5 leaves of gelatine,
  soaked in cold water
150ml (5fl oz) double cream
25g (1oz) icing sugar
½ teaspoon cinnamon

- Pour the wine, apple, orange and lemon juice into a saucepan, add the sugar and cloves and bring to the boil.

- Add the apple to the wine mixture and simmer for a few minutes until the apples are tender. Squeeze the water from the gelatine leaves before stirring them into the pan until dissolved. Leave to cool. Strain the jelly through a sieve into a jug, gently pressing the apple to release any juices, and divide among glasses or put into a pudding bowl. Refrigerate to set.

- Whip the cream in a small bowl with the icing sugar and cinnamon until soft peaks just form and it is thick enough to hold its shape. The cream can be spooned or piped on to the apple jelly or served separately.

bailey's crème brûlée

serves **six**

8 egg yolks
50g (2oz) caster sugar
450ml (16fl oz) double or
  whipping cream
150ml (5fl oz) Bailey's
2 tablespoons demerara
  or caster sugar

- Preheat the oven to 150°C/300°F/gas 2.

- Mix the egg yolks and sugar together in a bowl. Pour the cream and Bailey's into a saucepan and bring to the boil. Whisk the flavoured cream into the egg yolks and sugar.

- Ladle the mixture into six 7.5cm (3 inch) ramekins. Place them in a deep tray and pour in boiling water from the kettle so it reaches halfway up the ramekins. Cover the tray with foil and bake for 30–35 minutes until just set. To test, gently shake a ramekin. There should be a slight wobble in the centre of a set custard. Remove from the oven, take out the ramekins and leave to cool. Refrigerate to chill.

- Preheat the grill to very hot. Sprinkle the top of the custard with the sugar and place under the grill, watching carefully until the sugar caramelizes to a rich golden brown. Alternatively, a blowtorch can be used to caramelize the sugar.

pear macaroon crumble

serves **six**

1kg (2¼lb) ripe pears,
  peeled, cored and cut
  into large chunks
125g (4½oz) caster sugar
juice of 1 lime
200g (7oz) plain flour
100g (4oz) butter,
  cut into cubes
12 macaroons, crumbled
  into pieces

Almond macaroons are easily available to buy and add a different taste to this crumble with their crispy edge and chewy centre.

- Preheat the oven to 190°C/375°F/gas 5. Put the pears, 25g (1oz) of the sugar and the lime juice into a large saucepan and cook for a few minutes until softened. Spoon the pears and cooking juices into a 1.5–1.8 litre (2½–3 pint) pudding dish.

- Sift the flour and place in a food processor with the butter, blitzing until the mixture resembles fine breadcrumbs. Add the remaining sugar and mix again for a few seconds. Stir in the crumbled macaroons.

- Sprinkle the crumbs over the fruit without pressing down. Bake in the oven for 20–25 minutes until golden brown.

toffee pie with grilled bananas

serves **six**

225g (8oz) digestive biscuits
150g (5½oz) butter
4 tablespoons golden syrup
100g (4oz) caster sugar,
  plus extra for sprinkling
400ml (14fl oz) tin of
  condensed milk
200g (7oz) melted
  plain chocolate
3 bananas

- Preheat the oven to 180°C/350°F/gas 4. Crush the biscuits in a food processor or in a plastic bag with a rolling pin to crumbs. Melt 100g (4oz) of the butter and half the golden syrup together in a small saucepan and stir in the crumbs until well coated. Press the biscuit mixture into the base and sides of a 23cm (9 inch) loose-bottomed tart tin and bake for 10 minutes. Remove from the oven and leave to cool.

- Place the remaining butter and golden syrup, sugar and condensed milk in a saucepan and gently heat, stirring continuously, until all the butter has melted and the sugar dissolved. Bring to the boil, then reduce the heat to a simmer and stir for 8–10 minutes until light caramel in colour. Pour the filling into the biscuit case and leave to set.

- Pour and spread the melted chocolate over the surface of the caramel and refrigerate to set.

- Preheat the grill. Peel and slice the bananas in half lengthways. Lay the halves, cut-side up, on a baking tray, sprinkle liberally with caster sugar and grill until the sugar has caramelized to a golden brown colour.

- Divide up the pie and serve with the bananas.

and more

A sweet ginger cream is a tasty option to serve with this dessert. Whip together 150ml (5fl oz) double or whipping cream, 1 heaped tablespoon of icing sugar and a ½ teaspoon of ground ginger until soft peaks form. The biscuits for the pie base can also then be half ginger snaps and half digestives.

coffee and doughnuts

makes **six–eight**

75g (3oz) butter,
  cut into cubes
1 tablespoon caster sugar
150g (5½oz) plain flour
3 eggs
125ml (4fl oz) double cream
125ml (4fl oz) milk
2 tablespoons instant coffee
200g (7oz) milk chocolate,
  broken into pieces
1 instant custard cream
  (see page 372)
icing sugar, for dusting

This recipe involves a bit more work than others in the book, but these choux pastry doughnut rings filled with custard cream and topped with a coffee sauce are so delicious I couldn't leave them out. Once you've baked your choux pastry rings, the rest couldn't be easier.

- Preheat the oven to 200°C/400°F/gas 6. Put 200ml (7fl oz) water into a saucepan with the butter and sugar and heat until the butter has completely melted.

- Remove from the heat, sift the flour and add, beating vigorously to a smooth paste. Return to a low heat and stir continuously until the paste leaves the sides of the pan and forms a ball. Continue stirring for a few minutes before removing from the heat and leaving to cool for 3–4 minutes.

- Beat the eggs, one at a time, into the mixture until the paste is smooth and has a shiny finish (this can be achieved with an electric mixer using the beater attachment). Spoon the choux pastry, while still warm, into a piping bag with a plain nozzle.

- Grease a baking tray and cover with parchment or greaseproof paper. Pipe the choux pastry into six or eight rings, about 10cm (4 inches) in diameter, leaving a space between each. Bake in the oven for 30–35 minutes until well risen and golden brown. Transfer to a wire rack and cool completely.

- To make the sauce, bring the cream and milk to the boil and stir in the instant coffee. Lower the heat to a gentle simmer and stir in the milk chocolate until completely smooth.

- Split the doughnuts in half, spoon or pipe the instant custard cream into the base of each and replace the top. Lightly dust with icing sugar before serving with the warm coffee sauce.

and more

Cocoa powder can be dusted on top.

A splash of Tia Maria, Kahlúa or Bailey's can be added to the coffee sauce to enhance the flavour.

steamed simnel pudding

serves **six**

100g (4oz) butter
100g (4oz) caster sugar
2 eggs
1 egg yolk
200g (7oz) self-raising flour
50g (2oz) sultanas
50g (2oz) currants
25g (1oz) glacé cherries,
  chopped
25g (1oz) candied peel,
  chopped
75g (3oz) marzipan, cut
  into small cubes

Simnel is a fruitcake layered with marzipan traditionally served at Lent or Easter. I've taken all the flavours and transferred them into an easy steamed pudding, which can be made in the microwave. A jug of warm custard completes the dish.

- Lightly butter and flour a 1.2 litre (2 pint) pudding basin or six 150ml (5fl oz) moulds.

- Put the butter, sugar, eggs, egg yolk and flour into a food processor and blend until smooth. Remove the blade from the machine and fold in the fruits and the marzipan. Spoon the mixture into the basin and cover with the lid provided or clingfilm pierced with the point of a knife.

- Steam the pudding over boiling water for 1 hour 45 minutes or 40–45 minutes for individual puddings. Top up the water level as necessary during cooking.

- The pudding can also be cooked in a microwave. For a 500-watt oven, cook a large pudding on high for 5–6 minutes, or until a skewer pushed into the centre of the sponge comes out clean. For every 100 watts above this setting, take 15 seconds off the cooking time. Individual puddings will take approximately 2½–3 minutes.

kumquats suzettes

serves **four**

250g (9oz) kumquats
300ml (10fl oz) orange juice
175g (6oz) caster sugar
1–2 splashes of Grand
  Marnier, Cointreau
  or brandy
225g (8oz) plain flour
2 eggs
600ml (1 pint) milk

The oranges of the classic crêpes suzettes have been replaced here with small orange kumquats. The ease of this recipe lies in the fact that the kumquats and pancakes can be prepared and cooked well in advance, the sauce heated and the pancakes microwaved when you are ready to eat.

- Halve each kumquat and gently remove the small seeds. Pour the orange juice and sugar into a small saucepan with 150ml (5fl oz) water and bring to the boil. Add the kumquat halves, reduce the heat to a very gentle simmer and cook until tender. If the fruits are very ripe this may take only 20 minutes, but it can take up to 1½ hours. Once tender, add the liqueur.

- Sift the flour into a bowl. Add the eggs, pour in the milk and whisk until smooth. Heat a 20cm (8 inch) non-stick pancake pan. Lightly oil the pan, then ladle in just enough of the batter to coat the base thinly. Cook for 30–60 seconds until just set, flip over with a palette knife and continue to cook for a further 30 seconds. Slide the pancake on to a large plate and fold into quarters to create a triangle. Repeat this process until all the batter has been used to make 12–16 pancakes, covering with clingfilm.

- When you are ready to eat, reheat the pancakes in a microwave, divide among four plates and spoon over the warm kumquats. Serve with ice cream or cream.

orange flan with strawberries and orange curd cream

serves **eight**

3 eggs
100g (4oz) caster sugar
finely grated zest of
  1 orange
75g (3oz) plain flour
75g (3oz) ground almonds
½ teaspoon baking powder
100g (4oz) melted butter
8 tablespoons double or
  whipping cream
8 tablespoons orange curd
250g (9oz) orange
  marmalade
1–2 punnets of strawberries

- Preheat the oven to 190°C/375°F/gas 5. Generously butter a 20–25cm (8–10 inch) fluted tart tin. In an electric mixer or by hand, whisk together the eggs, sugar and orange zest until pale, thick and creamy. Sift the flour and mix together with the ground almonds and baking powder, then fold into the creamy mix. Slowly pour in the melted butter and fold in with a spoon. Pour the mixture into the buttered tin and bake for 12–15 minutes until risen, golden and spongy to the touch.

- Whisk the cream and orange curd in a bowl until soft peaks form.

- In a small saucepan, simmer together the marmalade and 100ml (3½fl oz) water until the marmalade is completely melted. The sauce can be strained or left chunky.

- Cut a wedge or spoon out a portion of the warm or cold flan, add some strawberries and drizzle over the warm sauce. Serve with a large spoonful of the orange curd cream.

and more

Icing sugar can be dusted over the flan before serving.

rhubarb and custard cheesecake

serves **eight–ten**

225g (8oz) digestive biscuits
100g (4oz) melted butter
450g (1lb) rhubarb, cut
  into 1cm (½ inch) pieces
200g (7oz) light soft
  brown sugar
juice of ½ lemon
3 leaves of gelatine,
  soaked in cold water
450g (1lb) cream cheese
250ml (9fl oz) ready-made
  instant custard, chilled
100ml (5fl oz) double
  cream, lightly whipped

The thin, bright sticks of rhubarb available between autumn and spring are the best to use, offering a rich colour and sweet flavour.

- Crush the digestive biscuits into fine crumbs (this can be achieved in a food processor) and stir in the butter. Press the mixture into the base of a 22–25cm (9–10 inch) loose-bottomed cake tin and refrigerate to set.

- Put the rhubarb and brown sugar into a saucepan and stir over a medium heat until thick and mushy. Add the lemon juice and liquidize in a blender or food processor to a smooth purée. Pour the purée into a bowl and stir in the gelatine until completely dissolved.

- Put the cream cheese and custard in the food processor and blend until smooth. Add the rhubarb purée and continue to blend until thoroughly mixed. Transfer the mixture to a large bowl and fold in the whipped cream. Pour the rhubarb cream on to the biscuit base, level the cream top until smooth and refrigerate for 2–3 hours to set before serving.

and more

A stewed rhubarb topping is not essential, but adds an extra fruitiness. Put 6 sticks of roughly chopped rhubarb into a saucepan with 3 tablespoons of caster sugar. Cook over a medium heat for several minutes until the rhubarb becomes tender, then leave to cool before serving on top of the cheesecake.

1–2 drops of grenadine can also be added to the rhubarb purée for a richer colour.

iced melon with mango, papaya and passion fruit

serves **four**

2 Charentais melons
6 tablespoons caster sugar
juice of 1 small lemon
1 mango
1 papaya
5 passion fruits

Charentais melons are the best to use here because their orange flesh gives a rich colour, but any melon will do. The iced melon crystals need to be frozen 6–8 hours before eating, but can also be made up to several days in advance.

• Chill a container for the melon crystals. Quarter the melons and remove the seeds. Cut away the skin, roughly cut the flesh and liquidize in a blender or food processor to a smooth purée.

• Gently warm the sugar and 6 tablespoons of water together in a small saucepan until the sugar has dissolved and the syrup boiled. Leave to cool. Mix two-thirds of the syrup with the melon purée and the lemon juice, pour into the chilled container and freeze for 6–8 hours, or preferably overnight.

• Peel the mango and papaya and remove the seeds from the papaya. Cut all the flesh into slices or cubes and chill until ready to serve.

• Halve four of the passion fruits and scoop out the seeds into a blender. Add the remaining syrup and blend until the seeds begin to break up, releasing the flesh. Strain through a sieve. Halve the remaining passion fruit and whisk the seeds into the strained syrup, then refrigerate until needed.

• Divide the mango and papaya among four plates and spoon the passion fruit syrup over. Scrape the frozen melon into crystals with a spoon, pile them on top of the fruit and serve immediately.

and more

1–2 teaspoons of grenadine can be added to the melon crystals for extra colour.

cracked raspberry meringue

serves **four**

2 egg whites
100g (4oz) caster sugar
1 teaspoon cornflour
1 teaspoon lemon juice
225g (8oz) raspberries,
  frozen and defrosted
  or fresh
50g (2oz) caster or
  icing sugar
1 tablespoon raspberry
  jam, at room temperature
1–2 punnets of fresh
  raspberries
clotted cream, to serve

- Preheat the oven to 140°C/275°F/gas 1. In an electric mixer, whisk the egg whites to a soft peak. Add half the caster sugar and whisk until approaching the stiff peak stage. Add the remaining caster sugar and continue to whisk until the meringue has a creamy consistency. Add the cornflour and lemon juice and whisk for a further minute.

- Very lightly oil a sheet of parchment paper and place on a baking tray. Spoon the meringue into four large mounds on the tray, leaving plenty of space between each. Bake for 50–60 minutes until the meringues are crispy. Remove from the oven and allow to cool.

- Put the 225g (8oz) of raspberries, sugar and jam into a blender and blend until smooth. Strain into a bowl.

- Arrange the meringues on plates and spoon the second batch of raspberries over and around. Drizzle with the raspberry sauce and complete with a scoop of clotted cream.

blackberry and almond tart

serves **six**

275–350g (10–12oz)
  ready-made shortcrust or
  puff pastry
3 tablespoons blackberry
  or blackcurrant jam
2 eggs
100g (4oz) caster sugar
100g (4oz) softened butter
100g (4oz) ground
  almonds
175g (6oz) blackberries

- Preheat the oven to 170°C/325°F/gas 3. Roll out the pastry on a lightly floured surface into a circle large enough to line a 23cm (9 inch) tart tin (preferably loose-bottomed). Lift the pastry on the rolling pin and place in the tart tin, easing the pastry into the bottom and corners of the tin and trimming off any excess overhanging pastry.

- Prick the base well with a fork. Spoon and spread the jam over the base of the case, then refrigerate for 20 minutes.

- In a food processor, blend together the eggs, sugar, butter and almonds until totally combined. Spread the almond mix into the tart case and place the blackberries on top.

- Bake the tart in the oven for 40–45 minutes until set and golden brown and eat warm or cold with pouring cream or ice cream.

index